Collective Bargaining
in the Public Sector

Emerging Issues in Employee Relations
John T. Dunlop and Arnold M. Zack, Editors

Grievance Arbitration
Issues on the Merits in Discipline, Discharge, and Contract Interpretation
Arnold M. Zack

The Management of Labor Unions
Decision Making with Historical Constraints
John T. Dunlop

A Handbook for Grievance Arbitration
Procedural and Ethical Issues
Arnold M. Zack

Turning the Tide
Strategic Planning for Labor Unions
David Weil

Collective Bargaining in the Public Sector
Morris A. Horowitz

Collective Bargaining in the Public Sector

Morris A. Horowitz

LEXINGTON BOOKS
An Imprint of Macmillan, Inc.
NEW YORK

Maxwell Macmillan Canada
TORONTO

Maxwell Macmillan International
NEW YORK   OXFORD   SINGAPORE   SYDNEY

in this case leave out P B 3

331.89
H81c

Library of Congress Cataloging-in-Publication Data

Horowitz, Morris Aaron.
Collective bargaining in the public sector / Morris A. Horowitz.
p.   cm.—(Emerging issues in employee relations)
Includes bibliographical references and index.
ISBN 0-669-21517-1
1. Collective bargaining—Government employees—United States.
I. Title. II. Series.

Lexington Books
An Imprint of Macmillan, Inc.0
866 Third Avenue, New York, N.Y. 10022

Maxwell Macmillan Canada, Inc.
1200 Eglinton Avenue East
Suite 200
Don Mills, Ontario, M3C 3N1

Macmillan, Inc. is part of the Maxwell Communication Group of Companies

Printed in the United States of America

printing number
1 2 3 4 5 6 7 8 9 10

Contents

Foreword

Governments are not only sovereigns, they are also employers. They confront many of the same problems in relating to their employees that private sector employers encounter. Employees need to be selected, hired, trained, compensated, motivated, disciplined, and, more generally, managed. This book is noteworthy because it delineates the wide range of issues that occupy governments in their roles as employers as well as the concerns of employees in their relations to government employers. In comparing private and public sector experience, the text also illuminates both. Professor Morris A. Horowitz brings to this dual opportunity a lifelong experience as a neutral in a variety of specific situations in both the private and public sectors.

But governments are not to be thought of as monoliths in their relations to their employees. There are the federal, state, county, and local governments; there is a wide array of agencies, occupations, and job classifications; there is a variety of organizational forms and managements including executive departments, independent agencies, and government corporations; their security sensitivity varies including military, foreign service, the CIA and FBI, and police and law enforcement; some occupations have a similar content to the private sector, and others are peculiar to governments. In the United States, these government employees currently number more than 18 million (3.0 million federal, 4.3 million state, and 11.0 million local), and aggregate government employment is growing.

The most fundamental difference between the public sector and the private sector in this country is derived from the separation and independence of the executive and legislative branches of government. The executive branch budgets, hires, and manages, but only the legislative branch can appropriate the money and authorize the taxes. (In a parliamentary government this separation is far less significant.) This separation generally applies in our federal, state, and local governments. As a consequence of this bifurcation, issues of wages and salaries, benefits, and employment for public employees are budget matters that require concurrence of both the executive and legislative branches of government, opening the gates for political conflict and providing an added incentive for political involvement by government employees. There is no general counterpart to this separation of powers in the private sector.

A more commonly noted difference between employment in the public sector and the private sector concerns procedures to determine union representation of public employees, to negotiate collective agreements that provide for a wide range of terms and conditions of employment, and to strike the public employer. While there are substantial differences between most public employment and the private sector in these respects, it is the limitations on the strike in the public arena that are most pervasive, although not universal in some states. The original rationale for this prohibition to strike was based largely on the powers of a sovereign. More recently the prohibition relies on the essential character of the services provided by government, and on the view that stark economic power used by public employees is not an appropriate means to influence political decisions on the allocation of public funds in a political democracy.

Professor Horowitz leads us through the decisions public employers of various types make respecting wages, fringe benefits, other terms and conditions of employment, and grievance handling and contract dispute resolution in collective bargaining with labor organizations. He helps us understand the differences between working and managing in the private sector and working and managing in various public employment settings with civil service rules. The discussion is well illustrated with examples and specific cases. The volume provides an insightful overview of collective bargaining in the public sector for professionals, government and union officials, students and citizens alike.

John T. Dunlop

Preface

The number of public employees in the United States has grown substantially over the past fifty years and currently constitutes 18.5 million, almost 17 percent of all nonagricultural employment. According to projections, aggregate employment in federal, state, and local government will continue to keep pace with the growth in private sector employment and will reach 21.5 million in the year 2005. This is a significant sector of our economy, currently exceeding total manufacturing employment.

Why is a special book necessary on industrial relations and collective bargaining for the public sector? The industrial relations system of any nation or society, or its sectors, may be analyzed in terms of three facets of the environment: the market context, the technology of the enterprise, and the power regulations of the enveloping society as reflected in the regulations specified by governments for the workplace.[1] Within these contexts, the participants—managers and their representatives, workers and their representatives, and regulators, who are generally agents of the government—interact with each other to determine the outcomes.

Although the public sector generally resembles the private sector in the range of technology, it differs in the contexts of market and power relations. The market as commonly understood in the private sector is absent from the public sector, which, instead, is constrained by executive- and legislative-determined budgets. The public sector generally functions as a form of monopoly, and competitive pressures arise from public groups exerting political influence, although some public services, such as the post office, are confronted by private alternatives. Further, there exists the legacy of an ideology that the sovereignty of government forbids bargaining with government employees; bargaining would be a surrender of sovereignty and an abdication of responsibility.

Despite these differences and special public sector problems, industrial relations systems have developed in the public sector that resemble in a number of ways the basic characteristics found in private sector industrial relations systems.

Public management has many of the same basic problems as does private management. The job of managers in both sectors is to manage the employees as efficiently and economically as possible: wages and benefits need to be determined; discipline standards are applied; workers need to be fired, promoted, transferred, and laid off. The daily problems that may arise among employees and between employees and their supervisors have considerable similarity in both the sectors. What differentiates public management is the political process. Unlike the private sector, management in the public sector is faced with a process in which the consumers—the electorate—have participatory rights in the problems of the workplace.

Chapter 1 examines some of the basic issues, such as the strike and wages, that differentiate public and private sector labor relations. It then highlights some of the other issues that differentiate the public and private sectors, such as the handling of grievances, the scope of bargaining, and the bargaining process versus the political process.

Chapter 2 details the history of public sector organized labor. Chapter 3 describes and analyzes wage determination in the public sector and makes comparisons with wage determination in the private sector. Chapters 4 and 5 cover monetary fringe benefits and nonmonetary contractual benefits. Chapter 6 looks at the resolution of disputes in the public sector, with some comparisons with the private sector. Chapter 7 describes public intervention in public sector bargaining, showing the differences between the public and private sectors. The concluding chapter summarizes the effective differences between the two sectors.

In order to highlight the differences between the public and private sectors, a number of chapters include Questions for Discussion and Case Studies sections. Many readers may have some understanding of collective bargaing in the private sector, and these questions and cases attempt to focus the readers' attention on the differences with the public sector. The case studies are a composite of situations with which I have become familiar over many years of exposure to collective bargaining in both the public and private sectors.

I thank John T. Dunlop and Arnold M. Zack, editors of the Emerging Issues in Employee Relations series. They both encouraged me in this effort and reviewed the manuscript, offering many helpful ideas and suggestions. I also thank Jennifer Dawson for typing and retyping the many drafts of the manuscript.

1

Public versus Private Sector Labor Relations

The Strike

Among the issues that differentiate public sector and private sector labor relations, the one that is often set forth as the most distinguishing factor is the strike. It is commonly accepted that public employees have no right to strike, whereas private sector employees do. In fact, however, there are some limits to the right to strike in the private sector. And although federal employees and most state employees are forbidden by law to strike, ten states since 1970 have granted the right to strike to public employees: Alaska, Hawaii, Illinois, Minnesota, Montana, Ohio, Oregon, Pennsylvania, Vermont, and Wisconsin. In none of these states is the right to strike unlimited; in all cases, a threat to the public health, safety, or welfare triggers a no-strike mechanism, and in most cases certain prestrike procedures must be followed. Moreover, essential services are protected in these states by provision of compulsory arbitration for some groups of employees.[1]

Where states do not have right-to-strike statutes, the courts have generally held that no such right exists. Nevertheless, thirty-eight states have no-strike laws on the books, and twenty-two of these specify penalties. Seven states (Connecticut, Florida, Iowa, Massachusetts, Michigan, Tennessee, and Vermont) grant employees the right to engage in "concerted activities" (generally interpreted in the private sector to include the right to strike) while simultaneously prohibiting strikes. And public employees in three states (Montana, Idaho, and California) have the right to strike without an explicit grant by statute. In these three states, actions by the courts have granted employees the right to strike.[2]

Public employees in most situations do manage to resolve problems that in the private sector would have meant a strike or a threat of a stoppage. The definition of what is essential service to the public may vary among situations and over the duration of the problem. One community may contract its trash collection to a private firm whose employees have the right to strike. Can a strike by the public employees of the neighboring community who do trash collection be forbidden? Should the school bus drivers of a private contractor have the right to strike but not the school bus drivers employed by the city? Should the city water meter readers not have the right to strike while electric meter readers employed by a private company have the right to strike? These types of questions are constantly arising, and frequently the answer is that the strike would be legal if the employer were not the government.

Over the years, public employees have engaged in strikes despite their illegality. In a study published in 1940, David Ziskind recorded 1,116 strikes by government employees.[3] Of those strikes, at least 63 had been in agencies whose function is public protection, 3 in public legislation and administration, 23 in public education, 94 in public health and sanitation, 72 in public road construction, 18 in public parks and recreation, 62 in public property maintenance, 114 in publicly owned utility operation, and 664 in the employment program of the Great Depression. Ziskind noted that one of the earliest strikes occurred in August 1835 when workmen in the Washington, D.C., navy yard struck for a change of hours and general redress of grievances; the men returned to work without any satisfaction. The following year, workers in the Philadelphia navy yard went out on strike for the ten-hour day that was common in the private shipyards, and the request was granted.[4]

The case for considering strikes by public employees as illegal appears stronger when the strikers are public safety employees—police officers and firefighters. Nevertheless, such strikes have occurred. As early as 1889, police officers in Ithaca, New York, went out on strike over a wage issue, and in 1918 the police of Cincinnati went out on strike. Many other strikes have occurred since then. A number of strikes by firefighters occurred early in

1890, four others were called in 1917, and many others occurred in 1918 and 1919.[5] It is clear that prohibitions against strikes have never by themselves prevented such action by government employees who regarded their grievances sufficiently great to lead them to assume the risks of the strike. One author notes, "Illegal strikes doubly damage that authority of the sovereign which the very denial of the right to strike seeks to preserve."[6]

The situations that have given rise to strikes by public employees have been similar to those of other strikes: a lag in wages compared to other workers in comparable employment or a lag in wages compared to the cost of living; a lag in various benefits or working conditions compared to other groups in either the public or private sector; the mishandling of various types of grievances; and autocratic-type management. What often differentiates a labor dispute in the public sector from that in the private sector is the uncertainty of the line of authority in the public sector, resulting in frustration and a strike. In a dispute by teachers over teaching schedules, who is the management representative who can negotiate with the teachers to reach a solution: the school principal, the superintendent of schools, the elected school committee, the city mayor, or the city council? The uncertainty, confusion, and delay may result in a strike, albeit an illegal one.

The strike in the federal government is prohibited by federal law and in other public sectors by a number of state statutes and court decisions. In general, public officials have supported the position that strikes by government employees cannot be tolerated. During the Boston police strike of 1919 Calvin Coolidge, then governor of Massachusetts, stated, "There is no right to strike against the public safety—by anybody, anywhere, at any time." In 1937 President Franklin D. Roosevelt wrote in a letter to the president of the National Federation of Federal Employees:

> A strike of public employees manifests nothing less than an attempt . . . to prevent or obstruct the operations of government until their demands are satisfied. Such actions looking toward the paralysis of government by those who have sworn to support it is [*sic*] unthinkable and intolerable.[7]

Despite the doctrine of sovereignty, the pronouncements by high and many lesser officials of government that government strikes are illegal, and the laws and court decisions declaring government strikes as illegal, strikes continue to occur. There is no uniform policy on strikes by public employees across the various levels of government, and in various government jurisdictions certain strikes are legal while others are not. Certainly not all strikes are legal in the private sector either. Some strike objectives are inappropriate and illegal, and certain strike methods and procedures have been held to be illegal. Certain services performed by private enterprise have been held to be essential in that strikes may imperil the national health or safety, and they have been restricted. Under the National Labor Relations Act, for example, it is an unfair labor practice for a union to strike in order to force or require an employer or self-employed person to join a union. And under the National Emergency provisions of the act, a strike may be delayed for up to eighty days while efforts are being made to resolve the dispute.

Could a uniform policy permit strikes of certain government workers while prohibiting such action by employees in essential government services? Such a dichotomy has been suggested, but other than police, fire, prison guards, and public community hospitals, what government services are essential to the health, safety, and welfare of the community? There is not likely to be unanimity on garbage collection, water works, and public utilities. How essential are transit employees in a large city, or teachers, or salespersons in state-owned liquor stores?[8] There undoubtedly are differences of opinion on what are essential services, and often the differences could be explored by ideology or by the situation in which the service is offered. How essential are garbage collectors in the winter, compared to a hot summer, and what if there are private contractors able to collect garbage? How essential are teachers in the summer or during the Christmas holidays? Can a service be considered essential if employees are providing the identical service in the private sector? There is also the matter of duration of a strike that may affect its legality. A five-day strike by custodians of public buildings, for example, may be acceptable, but a six-month strike by the same employees may be held illegal. In various situations, the length of the strike may determine how it is viewed by the public and the courts.

Whether strikes are in essential or nonessential services, or whether the strikes are legal or illegal, their purpose is basically different from that of private sector actions. Strikes in the private sector are designed to put economic pressure on employers; when a firm is deprived of revenue, the employer may face losses and even total economic disaster. However, the private employer has options: lock out its employees, hire replacements, or shut its doors and go out of business. Thus, both sides have some measure of economic power. In the public sector, a government agency or unit is not under the same economic and financial stress as a private employer. Instead, government officials are under political pressures by the public and their political constituencies to resolve the labor dispute and eliminate the inconvenience or disruptions of the strike.

Resolving the issue of the illegality of strikes in the public sector is not a simple matter. For a variety of reasons, strikes by public employees clearly raise issues concerning differences in the labor relations situation of the public sector compared to the private sector. When public employees do not have the right to strike what are the alternatives for the redress of grievances? If the only alternative is the political process, then this will shape the type of worker organization to emerge.

The Wage

A second basic issue that differentiates public and private labor relations is the wage and its determination. In the private sector, some companies pay a high wage while others in the same sector pay a low wage. And where employees are represented by a union, negotiations may take place on a company-wide basis or a plant-by-plant basis. Within any company or plant, there may be more than one bargaining unit, each of which may be negotiating for a different wage level and wage change. Where competition permits, a private company passes the costs of higher wages on to the consumer, in the form of higher prices. In many cases, the private company may have to absorb part of the wage increase out of greater productivity or profits.

In the public sector, wages, that is, the costs of public employees, are the major determinants of taxes, and they constitute approximately 70 percent of the costs of government. For most services rendered by the government the public has no choice; it must accept the service and pay directly for the product or pay taxes to cover the costs. Police and fire protection, prisons, tax collection, and libraries are basically monopoly services that the public cannot decide to forgo. The costs of these and other services are the bases for taxes, which the public is obliged to pay. Every wage increase for a government employee has an impact on the expenses of the government, unless offset, and potentially increases the need for taxes in the community. Increases in efficiency or reduction in service may reduce or affect the costs of a wage increase.

Government employees in classified positions—jobs in the principal units of government—generally have their wage set by the legislature through wage or salary scales, and employees move up this fixed structure based on time in the job and perhaps some other fixed criteria. The wage structure can be changed only by a legislative act. The wages of other government employees are fixed by the agency head, when there is no union, or by collective bargaining, when the employees are represented by a union. Regardless of how the wages are set, an increase means higher costs of government and a potential rise in taxes for all members of the community, unless the increase is offset by higher productivity or fewer employees.

The wage structure of government employees in classified positions, unionized or not, is generally changed through the political process of pressure on the legislature. Lobbying by unions, employee organizations, or informal employee groups may be effective in convincing a sufficient number of legislators to support a general wage increase. Government employees who are not represented by a labor organization may have to depend on political pressure on the agency head or legislative body for a wage change; even when they are represented by a union, the results of the collective bargaining process depend to some degree on political pressure on the agency head and on elected officials of the state or community.

There are no agreed-upon or commonly accepted policies that government managements utilize or invoke when faced with a demand for higher wages. What should the government policy be with respect to wage increase requests? Should government employees be limited to wage adjustments based on the adjustments or wage levels of similar government occupations in surrounding comparable communities? Should comparisons be made with private sector occupations in comparable communities? Government employees in the past have had greater tenure rights and job security than employees in the private sector. How much weight should be given to these factors when wage levels are being considered?

Another factor that may differentiate the public and private sector employees on the wage issue is the bargaining unit that defines the jobs and people grouped together for bargaining purposes. In the public sector, a state may employ groups as diverse as university professors, state police, building custodians, toll collectors, office clerks, and salespersons in state liquor stores. How many bargaining units should there be, and what wage relationship should exist among them? The need to answer such questions adds another factor that can differentiate the public and private sectors with respect to wages. If there are a substantial number of bargaining units in the public sector, the issue of the wage relationship among the various units is a matter that must be resolved, either in advance in a master plan or by an ad hoc approach, case by case.

A bargaining unit factor that may differentiate the public from the private sector is the issue of whether supervisors should be in the same unit as nonsupervisory employees. In the private sector, the National Labor Relations Act denies supervisors the bargaining rights extended to other employees, and as a result few supervisors join unions. In the public sector, supervisors historically have had close ties with the employees they supervise, and often shared work experiences and participation in the same employee associations. Many states permit first-line supervisors to be included in bargaining units with subordinates. A few states grant bargaining rights to supervisors but permit them to bargain only in units of supervisors. The federal government and a few states deny bargaining rights to supervisors.[9]

Handling of Grievances

The procedures for the handling of grievances in the private sector are normally specified in the collective bargaining agreement, and although there are variations in details, the basic process is the same: there are various steps in the process, and if the matter is not resolved, either party usually can refer the issue to an outside arbitrator, who is authorized to issue a final and binding award on the issue in dispute. A minority of bargaining agreements do not provide for arbitration as a final and binding step, and here the parties are ordinarily left to strike or implement a lockout in support of their position. In some agreements, the parties have specified certain issues that are not required to go to arbitration, and a strike may or may not be permissible. In other cases, the grievance procedure provides that the grievance is sent to arbitration only when both parties agree that arbitration is appropriate; otherwise, a strike is legal. When there is no collective agreement, an aggrieved employee ordinarily has no redress, except when a public law has been violated. In such a situation the employee may take the matter to an administrative agency or to the courts.

When a bargaining unit in the public sector is represented by a union, the grievance procedure is likely to be similar. However, there is also likely to be a civil service commission with some regulatory authority over the rules in the workplace, especially those involving hiring, promotions, transfers, and layoffs. In a unionized situation, a government employee in some states may have a choice of pursuing a grievance through the grievance procedure of the collective bargaining agreement or through the procedures of the civil service commission. In some jurisdictions a government employee can pursue a grievance through both procedures. In addition, when an issue involves the rules of an agency such as the Equal Employment Opportunity Commission (EEOC), an employee has the right to take the matter to that agency. Additionally, government employees not represented by a bargaining agent may have the civil service or EEOC procedures to pursue a grievance.

There is no uniform pattern of civil service rules and regulations among various political jurisdictions. Nevertheless, the existence of civil service commissions, with rules and regulations that affect government employees, clearly constitutes a further differentiation of public and private labor relations.

Management Problems

Public managers have the same basic responsibilities and problems as do private managers: the efficient and productive utilization of resources. On a day-to-day basis, there appears to be considerable similarity between the two groups of managers; however, the setting of the two sectors is sufficiently different so that the resolution and the process of resolving similar problems may be different.

In the private sector, management has ordinarily defined specific responsibilities, and the key measure of success is economic performance; if the department, plant, or company is profitable, the management is considered a success. Most units of the public sector do not have these same simple measures of success or economic efficiency. How do you measure managerial efficiency or success in a police department, a fire department, a department of public workers, or a municipal library? There may be measures of social welfare, but rarely can measures of economic efficiency and success be applied.

In many areas of the public sector, it is very difficult, if not impossible, to divorce measures of social welfare from measures of political expediency: almost all government agencies include political appointments in leadership posts, budgets of agencies are determined by political decisions, and agency programs and policies may be determined by political philosophy or opportunity. Politics also affects the basic management of day-to-day workplace problems. To be successful, public managers must consider the political consequences of any resolution of a workplace problem. They must be constantly aware that they are functioning in a political arena, so any significant action on their part will be judged from a political perspective. Indeed, political performance is often the standard by which a public manager is judged by the appointing or electoral authority.

Scope of Bargaining

In the private sector, the scope of collective bargaining covers wages, hours, and other conditions of employment, and over the years, this scope has been interpreted to cover most items that may affect the employees' compensation and welfare. The Labor-Management Relations Act, the National Labor Relations Board, and the courts have defined the scope of bargaining fairly broadly, and the issue of scope of bargaining is only occasionally a concern to unions in the private sector. Nonetheless, management rights questions and participation of workers in the enterprise are matters that may involve disputes over the scope of bargaining.

The scope of bargaining in the public sector is both more limited than that in the private sector and not uniform across the various political and geographic units (federal, state, and local) or even across bargaining units within a single political or geographic unit. The scope of bargaining is most limited in the federal sector, where wages, hours, and benefits, such as health and welfare and pensions, are legislated by Congress and administered by the Civil Service Commission. Hence, in the executive departments of the federal government, bargaining is limited to the number, type, and grades of employees, work methods and technology, and procedures for exercising managerial authority. In other federal agencies, such as the Postal Service, the naval shipyards, and the air traffic controllers, the scope is much broader, due to specific regulations of the government.

There is considerable variation among the states in legislating the scope of bargaining for state and local government employees, and in any single state, there may be variations in bargaining scope among different bargaining units. Classified employees are likely to have their salaries, hours, vacations, health benefits, and pensions set by state legislature, while other units may be free to bargain over these items. In some states, teachers are not permitted to bargain over the length of the school year or over the size of the class; in some jurisdictions, police and fire are prohibited from bargaining over certain specified subjects. Some states recognize no rights of government employees to collective bargaining.

Two basic aspects of bargaining scope differentiate the public sector from the private sector. One is that a single law, the National Labor Relations Act, covers the scope of almost all of the private sector (except railroads and airlines), while in the public sector, there are fifty state laws and a variety of federal laws covering the scope of federal government bargaining units. The second aspect of bargaining scope that differentiates the private and public sectors is the breadth of matters within the scope of negotiations. In the private sector, the scope of bargaining is broad, compared to government, while in the public sector scope varies but is still ordinarily narrower.

Bargaining Process versus Political Process

Another factor that differentiates labor relations in the private sector from those in the public sector is the effect of the political process on public sector labor relations. In the private sector, labor relations normally involves a relationship between a company management and the bargaining agent of the company's employees. An agreement between the two parties authorized by the two organizations is final, and if the parties agree to place a matter before an arbitrator, the arbitration award is final and binding. Occasionally an arbitration award is contested in the courts, but rarely is an award overruled. Awards have been overturned by the courts when an arbitrator is held to have exceeded his or her jurisdiction or the award contravenes public policy.

In the public sector, the bargaining process between the parties takes place in the context of a political process. That is, bargaining occurs between the two parties immediately concerned and also within the political arena. City managers and city councilors are often involved because of the political effects of any bargain struck by the immediate parties. It is not uncommon for one party or the other (although more likely the union) to appeal an unhappy resolution of negotiations to a higher political authority for redress, seeking additional conditions or benefits by legislation. Since public officials and legislators depend on public support for reelection, government employees may pressure the political hierarchy for a better settlement than reached through negotiations. The political process may provide a second step, after the bargaining process. This possibility of two bites at the apple clearly differentiates the labor relations in the private and public sectors.

In some political units, the governmental authority of funding is another factor differentiating the public from the private sector. If a bargaining agreement requires funding by a legislative body, as is ordinarily the case, the results of collective bargaining are not final until approved by that body. A public manager or executive may lobby the legislative body not to fund the agreement, thereby voiding the settlement and sending the parties back to the bargaining table.

A somewhat comparable situation may occur in the private sector when the negotiating committees of the parties reach a tentative agreement that the union membership fails to ratify. In such a situation, the parties are forced back to the bargaining table for further negotiations. (This development may also occur in a public sector bargaining situation.)

Despite some similarities, it is clear that the functioning of public sector labor relations in a political arena differentiates it from private sector labor relations.

Summary

Many of the day-to-day problems in the workplace are basically the same in the public and private sectors. However, many workplaces in the public sector involve distributive problems, and the options that public managers have available to resolve their problems are different because they operate in a political arena. Labor relations issues and their possible resolution differentiate the public sector from the private sector. Issues such as the strike, the determination of wages, the handling of grievances, and the scope of bargaining all involve political and public processes in some way and to a significant degree. Clearly, the overall picture of labor relations in the public sector is substantially different than that in the private sector. Its story must be told.

Questions for Discussion

1. How are public sector employee unions treated differently from private sector unions, and what is the rationale for the difference? Why is there a single national policy in private sector collective bargaining but not across the public sector? In view of the state-by-state handling of labor relations for state and local government employees, are these employees better off or worse off, compared to unionized employees in the private sector?

2. Why are almost all public sector employees forbidden to strike? Despite this prohibition, why have many public sector unions struck against government agencies? Why have the prescribed penalties for striking against the government not been effective in stopping public sector strikes? What policy could be used as a substitute for the strike?

3. Why is the scope of bargaining in the public sector more limited than in the private sector? What case can be made for having a uniform bargaining scope in both sectors? Does the merit system, commonly found in the public sector, require a more limited scope for public sector bargaining? If yes, in what ways?

4. Why is it more difficult to identify the "employer" in the public sector than in the private sector? Who are the possible players on the management side in public sector bargaining? Who has the final word for the employer in reaching an agreement with a union?

2

History of Public Sector
Organized Labor

The private sector in the United States has a long history of worker organizations for the purpose of maintaining or improving the wages, hours, and conditions of work. The first area to organize were skilled artisans—printers, shoemakers, and building tradesmen. General histories of labor and unions in the United States make no references to labor or unions in the public sector before the 1830s. One type of reference is in discussions of labor's drive for the ten-hour day in the early nineteenth century. In 1836 President Martin Van Buren issued an executive order establishing the ten-hour day "for mechanics and laborers on government works," after an appeal to the president by the National Trades' Union.[1]

Early History: Organizations and Strikes

Union organization and strikes in the public sector appear to have become an issue in the 1830s when the trade union movement began to struggle for the ten-hour day. A series of strikes and demonstrations in the private sector were relatively successful in attaining the ten-hour day. Where the ten-hour movement was successful, public authorities followed the lead of private employers, partly under public pressure and partly to maintain their skilled labor. In Boston, for example, where unions failed to gain the shorter day in private industry, the public authorities rejected the pressures to install the ten-hour day on public works. In Philadelphia, however, the shorter day was won in the private sector after a strike in 1835. Early in June 1835 the city employees went out on strike, and on June 4 the city council granted the shorter workday to its employees. Other public authorities in the vicinity quickly followed suit.[2]

Artisans employed by the federal government were not immediately as successful in gaining the ten-hour day. The mechanics of the New York and Brooklyn navy yards petitioned the secretary of navy for a reduction in hours, but unsuccessfully. In August 1835 the workers at the Washington, D.C., navy yard struck for shorter hours; the secretary of navy refused to yield, and the workers returned to work on the old terms. In June 1836, employees of the Philadelphia navy yard, the only establishment in the city where employees still worked longer than ten hours per day, struck for shorter hours. The action persisted for several weeks, and when the authorities refused to yield, the strikers sent a committee to President Andrew Jackson demanding the ten-hour day. The president acceded, and the shorter day was established for these federal workers. By October, the ten-hour day had been put into effect by executive action throughout Pennsylvania, New York, and Maryland in facilities where federal employees were organized. In those states and the District of Columbia where federal employees were not organized, the twelve- to fourteen-hour day continued to prevail.[3]

In March 1840, more as a result of a political concern than union pressure, President Van Buren issued an order making the ten-hour day the rule on all federal works, and this order was supplemented with a statement that the shorter day was not to be accompanied by a reduction in wages. This order changed the practice of having the government follow the labor standards of the private sector; the government became a leader in setting the labor standard in some communities.[4]

Despite this executive order and the general practice in federal works, problems arose in specific navy yards. An effort by the Navy Department to increase the day's work by one hour at the Charlestown, Massachusetts, navy yard in 1852 resulted in a strike of three hundred workers; after a few days, the order was revoked, and the workers returned to work. The issue of wages also rose in a number of government works, and strikes occurred.[5]

During the 1850s a number of the shipbuilding crafts in the private yards succeeded in obtaining an eight-hour day. As early as 1842, the authorities in the Charlestown navy yard accepted eight hours as a day's labor for ship's carpenters and caulkers engaged in repair and maintenance work.[6] By the outbreak of the Civil War, the eight-hour schedule was rather common in the private sector, which began attracting workers from a number of navy yards. There are no records of strikes to force the federal government to act, but in December 1861 Congress enacted a law (and amended it in July 1862) that established for employees in navy yards the policy of prevailing wage and prevailing practice.[7]

Union organizations and strikes in the public sector were not limited to the government navy yards. In 1863 in wartime, the bookbinders in the Government Printing Office, in Washington, D.C., went out on strike for wages equivalent to those prevailing in private print shops. The strike continued for seven weeks and was finally settled by a compromise. In 1868 the printers in the Government Printing Office went out on strike over the same issue, and the superintendent of public printing quickly came to terms.[8] Many of the army arsenals were organized by the same unions in comparable plants in the private sector. An early strike in the civilian employment of the army occurred at the Watervliet Arsenal, West Troy, New York, in 1893, when eighty mechanics struck for a change in wages and hours. The result of this strike remains unclear.[9] In 1899 the machinists struck the Rock Island Arsenal over wages and a series of grievances. Discussions were held between the secretary of war and officials of the International Association of Machinists over the strike, and a settlement appeared to have been reached. However, only about one-third of the strikers were reemployed, and these were discharged unless they consented to leave the union.[10]

In August 1911, a seven-day strike occurred at the Watertown Arsenal over the introduction of Frederick W. Taylor's scientific management procedures which involved fragmented tasks and a minute division of labor among workers through time studies. The workers agreed to return to work pending a congressional investigation of the Taylor system, which was subsequently precluded from government facilities by legislation. Even during World War I, public sector strikes continued to occur.[11]

Trade unionism, particularly among machinists, spread widely in the public sector by early in the twentieth century, and in 1904 the International Association of Machinists established District 44 to handle the affairs of government employees. During World War I the Metal Trades Department of the American Federation of Labor (AFL) changed its rules so as to permit all local unions at various navy yards and arsenals, whether they were strictly metal trades unions or not, to affiliate with local metal trades councils. In a short time, metal trades councils were established at nearly all of the navy yards and several of the arsenals. During World War I, when it was vital for the government to keep plants running smoothly and efficiently, orders were issued by the government virtually recognizing the unions, forbidding discrimination against their members, and directing the utmost cooperation with their representatives. This cooperative attitude, however, did not persist after the war.[12]

That employees in the public sector were different from those in the private sector was frequently an issue in the government's dealing with public employees. In 1902, for example, President Theodore Roosevelt issued an executive order forbidding federal employees to seek to influence legislation in their own behalf, "individually or through association, save through the heads of their departments." This so-called gag rule caused considerable unrest, defiance, threats, and even strikes. In 1912 Congress enacted the Lloyd–La Follette Act, which outlawed the gag rule and guaranteed the right of federal employees to organize and affiliate with outside labor organizations. The act was vague on the right of government employees to strike.[13]

In addition to navy yards, arsenals, and the Government Printing Office, which have employee counterparts in the private sector, the government also conducts industrial enterprises or services that have few equivalents in private enterprise—for example, the postal service and the police and firefighting services. In the postal service, free city delivery service was established in 1863, and in the same year the letter carriers of New York formed an organization. Within a decade, societies or associations of letter carriers were functioning in many larger cities. These groups were initially established as social organizations or benefit societies, but they soon turned to lobbying local politicians and congressmen to improve working conditions. The passage of the Civil Service Act of 1883 meant a merit system of appointment, and the letter carriers' dependence on politicians declined. This was the stimulus to change to trade unions. Through the efforts of the Knights of Labor, the carriers won the eight-hour day in 1888. Later the independent National Association of Letter Carriers was established.[14]

Attempts to organize post office clerks were made as early as 1879, and by 1888 the New York Post Office Clerk's Association had been established, designed to eliminate uncompensated overtime and to establish the eight-hour day. By 1890, various associations joined together to form the National Association of Post Office Clerks of the United States. In 1891 the railway postal clerks organized the National Association of Railway Postal Clerks, and in 1903 the rural letter carriers formed the National Association of Rural Letter Carriers.[15]

The early organizations of firefighters were fraternal and benevolent societies, but they soon took on some of the activities of trade unions. In 1903, the American Federation of Labor chartered the first firefighters' union in Pittsburgh. This was established as a federal union, and by 1918 fifty-six separate firefighters' federal unions sent delegates to Washington, where they formed the International Association of Fire Fighters (IAFF). The right of firefighters to join a labor union and to affiliate with the trade union movement was challenged in many cities. There were a number of strikes prior to 1918, and the number of strike threats, strikes, and lockouts increased significantly in 1918 and 1919. Some strikes were successful; some were not. Despite defeats and setbacks, trade unionism among firefighters continued to expand until September 1919, when the Boston police strike reversed the trend. A wave of hostility to the unionization of municipal employees swept the country. Approximately fifty IAFF locals withdrew from the organization or failed to maintain good standing within the next year. Nevertheless, strikes by firefighters continued on into the 1930s.[16]

Police organizations, generally benevolent associations, spread through many cities in the second half of the nineteenth century, with some tracing their history back to pre–Civil War days. Many engaged in lobbying for legislation and policies favorable to police. A few police organizations applied to the AFL for union charters, but they were refused because of an AFL policy refusing admission of an organization of police. There were two recorded early police strikes, but most police organizations hesitated to strike. Shortly after World War I, there was pressure in many cities for wage increases, and early in 1919 the AFL lifted the twenty-year-old barrier against chartering police unions.[17]

Despite the opposition of the police commissioner, the Boston police organization applied for an AFL charter, and on August 8, 1919, the charter was granted. The commissioner contended that policemen were not employees but officers of the state, and he forbade them to belong to any organization affiliated with a body outside the department. Negotiations on the matter took place at the political level, and an apparent agreement was reached. However, before the agreement was released to the press, the police commissioner suspended nineteen members of the police union for violating the departmental regulation. The union voted by 1,134 to 2 to strike the following day, September 9, 1919, at 5:45 P.M. Violence and considerable rioting occurred, and on September 11, Governor Calvin Coolidge called out the state guard. Disturbances and violence continued in the streets of Boston, and despite support of the strike by other Boston unions, the strike was lost. The Boston public, and the public at large across the nation, generally opposed the strike. The union was smashed, and more than eleven hundred police officers lost their jobs. Governor Coolidge's statement— "There is no right to strike against the public safety by anybody, anywhere, at any time"—appears to have made him a national hero. The strike not only destroyed trade unionism among the police for a generation but dealt the movement among other public sector employees a serious setback.[18]

Despite the illegality of public employee strikes in most government jurisdictions, such strikes continued to occur. The number of public employee strikes, most of them illegal and among local government employees, rose dramatically in the late 1960s and continued at a high level through 1980. In the federal sector, the largest number of strikes recorded in one year was five in 1962; through 1980, the number varied between three and one. The total number of strikes in the public sector (federal, state, and local governments) declined substantially in 1981, and throughout the 1980s the number continued to decline.[19]

This brief history of early union organization and strikes in the public sector indicates a number of significant features. Although public sector employees did not appear to organize as early as workers in the private sector, this contrast was probably not due to ideological reasons. The artisans in the private sector were first to organize, and other groups, in both the private and public sector, followed. Although there was some early opposition to unions in the public sector, such as in the navy yards, the government subsequently recognized such unions and dealt with them. At the local level, police and firefighters organized, and although there was opposition in some communities to the idea of safety workers (police and fire) organizing into unions, other communities accepted such organization. Strikes were called by many different groups of public sector employees. They won some and lost some, and in most instances, the key issues were economic ones. Just as in the private sector, some public sector unions grew and continued in existence for a long period, while others seemed to have had a brief existence. The Boston police strike of 1919 appears to have resulted in a basic change in the public sector. It aroused a widespread public animosity and opposition to unions in the public sector. The issue of the right of public employees to organize into unions came to the forefront, and the legal differentiation between public and private sector employees was sharpened. The right of public employees to strike became a public issue. Over the years, strikes in the private sector became more permissive, while strikes in the public sector became more restrictive.

Public sector unions were sensitive to the matter of differences between the public and private sectors. Whether the differences were real or merely perceived, there undoubtedly was a general feeling in the political arena that public employees were different from those in the private sector. Although some public sector unions did not appear to be inhibited in their union activities, others publicly showed a sensitivity to the public perception. In 1930, for example, the constitution of the IAFF was changed to read: "We shall not strike or take part in any sympathetic strike."[20] In 1940 the president of the American Federation of State, County, and Municipal Employees (AFSCME) declared:

> It is our feeling that it should not be necessary to resort to strikes and that problems affecting government employees should be solved

through legislation and by negotiations with and cooperation with state and local government officials. In our opinion it is not a proper exercise of power for public employees to use the strike method to gain their ends.[21]

Despite various expressions of opposition to strikes and of support of the dependence on the political process, strikes by public employees continued to occur. Shortly after the president of AFSCME made this statement indicating opposition to the resort of strike, AFSCME came to the support of its locals in strikes on three occasions—one in Philadelphia and two in Buffalo. In 1946 there were a number of strikes by AFSCME locals in cities of over ten thousand and threats of strikes in many more.[22]

Professional Organizations in the Public Sector

Many of the early unions in both the private and public sectors had their origins as benevolent associations for mutual assistance of members in times of emergency. Recognizing the importance of economic issues, many of these associations gradually evolved into organizations that had many or all of the characteristics of trade unions. This was a common phenomenon in the private sector, where collective bargaining was generally acceptable, particularly in some industries and in some occupations. It was also common in some public sector services, such as navy yards and arsenals, where artisan occupations were the same as or equivalent to those in the private sector. In those parts of the public sector where collective bargaining was not generally accepted, employee associations continued in existence for a longer time period as an association for public sector employees.

In general, there were two broad types of employee organizations in the public sector. The simple professional association, comprising teachers or nurses, was concerned largely with professional standards and accreditation. Membership of these associations generally included management and administrative personnel who met the qualifications of the profession. A second type of employee association was that united by a common employer, such as a state employee organization, and it generally accepted management and administrative personnel as members. Prior to the 1960s most of these organizations of both types shunned collective bargaining. The single professional organization spent considerable effort to raise qualification standards for their profession, thereby making the profession more valuable to the employees and to management. Lobbying the appropriate legislature for various benefits for the profession was an important activity. The state employee organizations engaged mainly in lobbying the legislature for improvement in wages and other benefits.

President John F. Kennedy's executive order 10988 in 1962 set a different tone for federal employee organization, and union activities of the 1960s appear to have changed the focus of many of these employee associations and their attitudes toward unionism and collective bargaining. After the 1960s many of the single professional associations became more like unions themselves and engaged in collective bargaining. Others, especially the state employee associations, merged with unions in order to survive. The evolution of some government employee associations into unions and the absorption of others by established unions played a major role in the growth of public sector unionization.[23]

In the recent growth of unionization in the public sector, professional associations, such as the Professional Nurses Association, the National Education Association, and the American Association of University Professors, together with various police and fire associations, have played the role of "new unions."[24] That is, they began to engage in collective bargaining. The significant growth spurt after 1960 of unions in the public sector was a result of these various factors. Public employees' attitudes appear to have changed significantly in favor of unions. The public sector continued to attract younger workers and members of minority groups, and in many cities civil rights and public sector union movements became intertwined. Many employee organizations changed their policies in regard to collective bargaining in order to attract or retain members. In addition, the labor movement in general appears to have begun to pay more attention to unionization in the public sector, and some private sector unions provided direct assistance to public sector organizations.[25] Despite these rapid changes, in 1972 there still were over forty independent associations of civil service employees operating on a statewide basis and having an industrial-type membership. More than half of these had been in existence for twenty-five years or more, and almost one-quarter had been in existence for thirty-five years or more.[26] As a result of these changes, by 1989 membership of state employee associations of general government workers totaled fewer than two hundred thousand and state associations of school employees totaled only slightly more than one hundred thousand.[27]

Evolution of Collective Bargaining

Despite the absence of laws specifically prohibiting the process of collective bargaining by public employee organizations in the nineteenth century, the gains made were generally through lobbying and political pressures. Where there appeared to be a direct tie-in between private employees and public employees (such as between private shipyards and navy yards) in the same community, public employees generally obtained the same or similar benefits that the private employees managed to get through strikes or collective bargaining. However, because of a variety of reasons, including the belief that the state would be undermined if it bargained with its employees, collective bargaining in the public sector rarely occurred until the post–World War II period.

Up until the 1880s public employee organizations depended largely on lobbying to gain benefits and favorable legislation and policies. The federal Civil Service Act of 1883 created a merit system, and state legislatures followed suit. There was no longer the same impetus for political action by public employees covered by a merit system. By the early twentieth century unionism had spread widely in the public sector.

In a 1990 study of collective bargaining agreements (those covering one thousand or more workers), the U.S. Bureau of Labor Statistics found that there were 1,922 agreements covering 8.8 million workers; of these, almost 6 million (69.6 percent) were in the private sector, and 2.5 million (30.4 percent) were employed by state and local governments.[28] Thus, although employment in the public sector represented about 16 percent of total nonagricultural employment, union membership in the public sector represented 30 percent of total union membership. Marked changes occurred immediately prior to and after World War II, and despite public concern about unions in the public sector, strikes in both sectors increased substantially immediately after World War II. In 1946 Virginia passed a law banning strikes in the public sector, and in the following year eight other states followed suit. In that same year the Taft-Hartley Act was passed, banning strikes in the federal service and making such actions a possible felony. In general, the penalties in these state laws tended to be stiff, ranging from termination and ineligibility for reemployment for twelve months, to definition of striking as a misdemeanor, and to fines and imprisonment.[29]

The most important right that may be granted public sector employees in a bargaining environment is the right to bargain. These employees thereby have the right to form and join a labor organization, and the public employer is required to bargain with representatives of the employee organization. This right did not come about to any degree until the 1950s and early 1960s when a number of states passed laws establishing the right of employees to join employee organizations, and most of these laws authorized employers to bargain collectively or to meet and confer. In some states, collective bargaining in the public sector was authorized, but it was on a permissive basis,[30] that is, either party could refuse to bargain.

The breakthrough that is generally seen as critical for pervasive change in public and legal attitude toward unions and collective bargaining in the public sector was the issuance of executive order 10988 by President Kennedy in 1962, which established rudimentary bargaining rights for federal employees. According to one source, during the 1960 presidential campaign, the postal union leaders were successful in extracting a pledge from Kennedy that if elected, he would support bargaining by postal and other federal employees.[31] Lack of congressional support for this led Kennedy to issue executive order 10988, establishing a labor-management relations program for federal executive branch employees. This order provided for only a limited scope of bargaining and did not create a central administrative agency, but as a first step, it was regarded by postal unions and other federal employee unions as their Magna Carta.

This legalizing of unionization in the federal sector had ramifications in other parts of the public sector and apparently started a movement among many states to permit or authorize collective bargaining for state and municipal employees. In the federal sector, the impact of the executive order was strong; it had the effect of legitimizing formal negotiating procedures, unit determination exclusive recognition, and unfair practice procedures.[32]

A significant factor that differentiates collective bargaining in state and local governments from that in the private sector is the wide diversity of workplaces the average public employer must deal with. In a single state, public management must negotiate with such diverse groups as state police, bridge and tunnel toll collectors, highway department employees, university professors, prison guards, state liquor store employees, and clerical, technical, and professional employees under the state civil service system. A single municipality may have to negotiate with such diverse groups as police, firefighters, sanitation workers, teachers, school bus drivers, public works employees, and clerical, technical, and professional employees in city hall. Such diversity undoubtedly complicates the role of the public sector manager who has the responsibility of negotiating and bargaining with these groups. In the private sector, some employers may have to deal with a number of diverse craft unions. However, in most private sector situations, the employer would not be bargaining with such diversified bargaining units.

Recent Developments in Collective Bargaining

Favorable stage legislation for collective bargaining for state employees began with a 1955 Wisconsin statute, which was expanded in 1962 to cover municipal employees in the state. This law provided for a central administrative body, similar to the National Labor Relations Board (NLRB) to enforce and apply policies and procedures and for a means to resolve impasses through mediation and factfinding.[33] By the end of the 1960s, most industrialized states had enacted laws favorable to collective bargaining for public employees. Federal employees, however, were not completely satisfied with their procedure compared to those in a number of states, and this dissatisfaction led to the issuance in October 1969 of executive order 11491 by President Nixon. This order did not broaden the scope of bargaining, but it did establish a centralized administrative structure, which was seen as a marked improvement by nonpostal federal employees. Postal workers were unsatisfied, and after a successful strike for improved economic benefits and a new bargaining structure similar to that in the private sector, the 1970 Postal Reorganization Act was passed. This law established the Postal Corporation and placed its labor relations activities under the private sector Labor-Management Relations Act. The scope of bargaining was broadened greatly but had specific exemptions for pensions and for some personnel actions; compulsory union membership was prohibited, and in place of the right to strike, unions were given the right to take "interest" disputes to arbitration.[34]

During the first generation of public sector bargaining, the economy was expansionary, as was the legal environment. Between 1960 and 1975, some thirty-eight states adopted legislation providing unionization and bargaining rights for public employees, while only one such law existed in 1959.[35] By the mid-1980s collective bargaining in the public sector had come of age. The federal government, the District of Columbia, and all but two states authorize and require collective bargaining either for government employees generally or for specific categories of such employees. The federal government and a significant number of states have single statutes applicable to collective bargaining by all government employees; the remaining statutes have one or more laws dealing with specific categories of government employees. These statutes cover virtually all government employees at the state and municipal levels.[36]

Another differentiating factor between the private and public sectors is the scope of bargaining—that is, the range of issues that may be or must be negotiated by the parties to a collective bargaining agreement. In the private sector, the NLRB and the courts have defined scope to cover wages, hours, and conditions of employment. In the public sector, the scope of bargaining is not as broad and may vary among government jurisdictions. The most limited scope is found in the federal government, where the wages of federal classified employees are determined not by collective bargaining but by the Pay Comparability Act of 1970. The Federal Civil Service Reform Act of 1978 makes it unlawful to bargain over most employee benefits, hours, holidays, leave pay, and the classification of positions.

In the public sector outside the federal government, pressures grew to expand the scope of bargaining, and as the 1970s progressed, the confusion and controversy over competing systems— civil service and merit laws on the one hand and the scope of bargaining on the other—lessened. The trend was to consider most topics bargainable, so wage, hours, and condition items were shifted into the scope of bargaining. Currently most states have no statutory provisions limiting the scope of bargaining; most laws simply impose on the parties the duty to bargain with respect to "wages, hours, and other terms and conditions of employment."[37] Thus, although most state laws seem to make pay a negotiable item, most civil service laws provide such benefits as sick leave, holidays, health and life insurance, and retirement plans. In some bargaining units, issues arise that are not clearly in the scope of collective bargaining yet have a direct and sometimes significant impact on the conditions of employment. These issues are sometimes resolved by arbitrators through the grievance procedures specified in agreements; in some cases, the matters are resolved by the state courts.

Impact of Budgets

Until the 1980s public sector unions were expanding and at the same time were negotiating improved benefits at a faster pace than their counterparts in the private sector. But the atmosphere changed during the 1980s as many states and communities began facing increasingly serious budget problems. There appeared to be a growing public opposition to increasing taxes and fees, making it more and more difficult for public sector unions to negotiate wage and benefit packages.

By the beginning of the 1990s, state and local budgets were being trimmed. The public appeared strongly opposed to raising taxes, and because of economic conditions throughout the nation and the attitude of the federal administration to state and local aid, many state and local services had to be cut. Some public employees faced no increases in benefits. In addition, the time-honored tradition of job security for public service employees was being changed in the face of budget deficits in many communities; public employees were faced with the dilemma of wage reductions or layoffs. In not every situation were public sector unions given the choice. Wage changes had to be negotiated, but public management did not always need union approval to reduce the work force.

Public sector unions have faced the mounting budgetary crisis in different ways. Some unions, arguing safety or working standards, have fought hard to prevent layoffs. Others have been willing to accept layoffs in a trade-off for a wage increase or for no wage reduction. A growing number of public sector unions are likely to continue facing such dilemmas in the near future.

Questions for Discussion

1. What is the rationale for treating public employee unions differently from private sector unions? Why is there a single national policy in private sector collective bargaining but not in the public sector? In view of the state-by-state handling of labor relations for state and local government employees, are these employees placed at a disadvantage compared to unionized employees in the private sector?
2. Why are most public sector employees forbidden to strike? Why have many public sector employee organizations struck against government agencies despite the prohibition? Why haven't the prescribed penalties for striking against the government been effective in stopping public sector unions from striking? What policy could be used as a substitute for the strike?
3. Why is the scope of bargaining in the public sector generally more limited than the scope of bargaining in the private sector? What case can be made for having the same wider bargaining scope in both sectors? Does the merit system, found in most public sector employment, require a more limited scope on public sector bargaining? If yes, in what ways?
4. Why is it more difficult to identify the "employer" in the public sector than in the private sector? Who are the possible players on the management side in public sector bargaining? Who has the final word for the employer in reaching an agreement with a union?
5. Why have public sector employee organizations grown more rapidly than private sector unions recently? Have public sector unions done as well financially for their members as have private sector unions? If bargaining scope is limited in the public sector, how do the unions make gains in such benefits as retirement and health insurance?

3

Wage Determination

In the private sector, the key issue in collective bargaining, which normally takes top priority, often involves the wages of the workers in the collective bargaining unit: how much of a wage increase will employees receive? Occasionally there will be demands to change the wage structure or to establish a new hiring-in rate, or a new or improved benefit, or for a "give back" in work rules or benefits, but the wage issue is normally critical. Although the union negotiating team must take the settlement back to its membership for ratification, it is an infrequent occurrence, say once in eight or ten cases, for the membership not to ratify the negotiated settlement. On the management side in the private sector, it is even less likely for a negotiated settlement to be turned down by the company management, since ordinarily a tentative proposed agreement is cleared in advance with the small group of management that has the authority to accept or reject the terms. Unlike the union, the company does not function as a democracy, although associations of companies that bargain together may have procedures for ratification that encounter some problems in achieving ratification.

Collective bargaining in the public sector is different in a number of significant ways. The question of who bargains, for what, with whom, and why is not only of academic or legal interest; the answers to questions regarding the authority to bargain for the employers, the composition of the bargaining unit, the scope of bargaining, and the legal rules for playing the game often predetermine the results of bargaining.[1]

The Right to Organize and Bargain

The most important right granted to public employees is the right to bargain. Those employees also have the right to form and join a labor organization, and the public employer is required to bargain with representatives of the organization. For the employees of states, cities, and towns, this right did not come through until the 1950s and early 1960s, when a number of states passed laws establishing the right of public employees to join employee organizations. These laws generally authorized employers to bargain with employee organizations or to meet and confer with them. In some states, collective bargaining in the public sector was authorized but on a permissive basis.

In 1955 Wisconsin became the first state to authorize collective bargaining for state employees, and in 1962 the law was expanded to cover state municipal employees. By the end of the 1960s, most industrialized states had enacted laws favorable to collective bargaining for public employees, and by 1975, thirty-eight states had adopted legislation providing unionization and bargaining rights for public employees. By the mid-1980s all but seven states had statutes dealing with collective bargaining for one or more groups of government employees.

In the federal sector, the breakthrough for bargaining rights came in 1962 when President Kennedy issued executive order 10988, establishing rudimentary bargaining rights for federal employees. This executive order provided for a limited scope of bargaining, but it had a strong impact on organizing of federal employees. It apparently also started the movement in many states to permit collective bargaining for state and municipal employees. In 1969 President Nixon issued executive order 11491, which improved the bargaining rights of federal employees by establishing a centralized administrative structure. The postal workers were not satisfied, however, and after a successful strike for improved economic benefits, the 1970 Postal Reorganization Act was passed. This statute established the Postal Corporation and placed its labor relations activities under the private sector Labor-Management Relations Act.

The right to organize and bargain collectively in the public sector came about twenty years after this right was granted to private employees. In the private sector, all employees other than railroad and airline workers were covered by the same law and administrative agency. In the public sector, the federal government and the states passed their own statutes, at different times and with separate procedures and administrative agencies. The coverage of employees with the right to organize varies among the states. There is no uniformity among the states in the coverage and bargaining rights of public sector employees.

Scope of Bargaining

In the private sector, bargaining over wages, hours, and conditions of employment has been interpreted broadly, and few items affecting earnings or benefits are excluded from the scope of collective bargaining. In the public sector, certain items may be precluded from the collective bargaining process by legislative determination. Government employees in classified positions—that is, jobs in the principal units of government—generally have their wages set by the legislature. Wage or salary structures are established by law, and employees move up the structure based on some fixed criteria, such as time in the job. Changes in the structure occur by legislative act or by a formula established by legislation. For other government employees, wages are fixed by the government agency head (when there is no union) or by collective bargaining (when the employees are represented by a union).

In the federal sector and in some states, laws prescribe that wage levels be set in accordance with the standard of comparability to wages received by private employees performing similar work. This standard plus budget stringencies have often limited the wages of government employees to lower levels. The fact that wage determination is excluded from the scope of collective bargaining for specified groups in the public sector does not mean that the employees affected, or the employee organizations affected, have no leverage. It is not uncommon for the public sector unions to seek to influence legislatures directly on wages and other benefits by lobbying and political action. They may also affect wages indirectly, by becoming involved at various stages in studies and determinations of comparable wages. These organizations have a vested interest in having wage surveys show higher wages, and therefore considerable lobbying and pressure goes on so that results may be favorable to the labor organizations.

In some localities, and probably in some states, the public sector unions are sufficiently large that they may be considered a significant political force that elected officials must take into consideration. At the local level especially, union members and officials may live side by side with government elected officials. They are neighbors and sometimes friends. In communities where unions join together in a common cause for a wage adjustment, this may involve a significant vocal group of citizenry who are likely to vote in an election. Thus, when unions of police officers, firefighters, sanitation workers, teachers, and other general municipal employees join together in a lobbying effort for economic gain, the political pressures may be effective. However, if higher taxes result, there could be a rise in public resentment to the gains of government employees.

While such joint action may result in a significant economic gain, and in some cases, one may argue, in an unwarranted economic gain, the occurrence of joint lobbying activities and their success are not that frequent. Depending on the size of the community and its political situation, the form of government, and the relationship between the executive and legislative bodies, joint union power can vary significantly among communities. Had such cooperation among public sector unions in a locality been a successful tactic, it undoubtedly would have become more common, but it has not become a pattern. Few localities have a formal council of public sector unions that coordinates the collective bargaining with the single public sector employer.

The Federal Employees Pay Comparability Act of 1990 (Public Law 101-509, sec. 529, November 15, 1990) made some basic changes in pay adjustments for federal employees. The act adopted the concept of locality pay for federal white-collar employees paid under the General Schedule (G) pay system. Unlike the previous requirement that G salary rates apply nationwide, the act specifies that rates will vary depending on prevailing nonfederal salary levels in each locality where federal employees work. Locality-specific salary adjustments are to be made in each pay area where overall federal salary rates are more than 5 percent behind nonfederal rates for the same level of work. The act specifies that salary adjustments by locality are to begin in 1994 and that G employees in all pay areas are to be no more than 5 percent behind their nonfederal counterparts by the year 2003. Under the act, the Bureau of Labor Statistics is responsible for gathering nonfederal pay data to be used to determine the size of the federal-nonfederal pay disparities by pay area. These salary adjustments are in addition to the annual adjustments that all white-collar employees will receive under the act, based on changes in the private sector wage and salary Employment Cost Index, a measure of private sector pay increases during a one-year period. The president retains the authority to modify or deny either of these adjustments when he determines there is a national emergency or serious economic conditions affecting the general welfare. President Clinton has proposed to freeze wages in 1994.

For most public sector employees, retirement and pension plans are also mandated by law and therefore are excluded from the collective bargaining process. In addition, many states set vacations, holidays, and holiday pay for all or some of their employees, thereby precluding these items from the bargaining process. In some jurisdictions, teachers are precluded from bargaining over size of class or over their hours of work or work schedule. The hours of work and work schedules of some public sector employees are set by legislature in some political jurisdictions. In some instances, firefighters may be precluded from bargaining over the number of employees required on each shift.

Unlike the situation in the private sector, where the scope of collective bargaining is very wide and is uniform across the nation, public sector collective bargaining is generally more limited in scope and varies substantially among the states and between the states and the federal government. It is not easy to determine whether because of these differences employees in the private sector are better off than those in the public sector. In some jurisdictions, the legislated wages and benefits are higher than those attained by private sector employees through the collective bargaining process; however, there is variation among the states and also over time. In some periods, public sector employees on average do not do as well as private sector employees. This has been especially so during the early 1990s, when the general public has reacted strongly against increasing public expenditures and increasing taxes.

Separation of Powers in Government

In a number of states and many localities, public sector collective bargaining is not authorized. But even where authorized, one aspect of the public sector that may affect negotiations is the separation of powers in government between executive and legislative branches. Where collective bargaining is authorized, the executive branch normally has the primary responsibility for appointing a representative to negotiate with the union. The legislative body, however, has the power of the purse, so any agreement reached that requires funding typically requires some approval by this body. If it is not limited by statute, the legislative body may accept or reject the proposed agreement by funding or not funding it. If it rejects a proposed agreement, the parties to the negotiations have no alternative but to go back to the bargaining table. Nevertheless, as is true in any political forum, much lobbying and political maneuvering may take place before the legislative body takes final action.

Public employee unions, particularly at some state and local levels, do have political influence, and it is infrequent that a tentative agreement reached at the bargaining table is rejected by the legislative body. This is true in part because the executive has entered into the agreement and is expected to support the agreement. In some situations, especially at the local level, one or more representatives of the legislative body may be asked to participate on the management negotiating team to forestall a possibility of legislative nonsupport after a tentative agreement is reached.

This division of authority between the executive and legislative branches may vary from state to state and among localities. In Massachusetts, for example, some communities are governed by elected selectmen, and in some cases all of the selectmen participate in the negotiation with the public sector unions. When an agreement is reached at the bargaining table, there is little likelihood that the agreement would not receive funding. However, if only a minority of selectmen participate in the negotiations, even when a majority of the management negotiating team agrees on the terms of a contract, a majority of the total body of selectmen may not approve funding for the contract.

When a hired town manager negotiates for a community and then must take the agreement to an open town meeting for approval, there is always the possibility of rejection. Here, the politicking of the union members among the citizenry who attend the meeting may be crucial. Where a city mayor or representatives negotiate for management, the city council, as the legislative body, must give its approval of the agreement. Thus, although officials in the executive branch generally negotiate agreements with employee representatives, the legislative body of the community holds the budget and taxing powers and thereby the authority not to fund a settlement.

Civil Service Merit System

The civil service merit system also has an impact on labor relations with public sector employee organizations. The theory behind the merit system is that public employees will be hired, fired, promoted, and paid on the basis of merit and that the merit principle will be protected by a commission that is independent of the public employer. The merit principle is such that personnel matters should depend solely on a person's merit, with no consideration given to personal or political support; in other words, within the civil service, public employees are to be recruited, selected, and advanced under conditions of political neutrality, equal opportunity, and competition on the basis of merit and competence. The merit system is any formally established set of procedures designed to implement the merit principle.

The first merit system in the United States was enacted in 1883 by the passage of the Pendleton Act. This basic federal civil service reform law was followed by similar legislation on the state and local levels. By 1970 the merit system at the federal level covered 89 percent of its civilian employees, and at least some of the employees in all the states were under a merit system.[2]

Over the years, there has been some concern that the merit system is threatened by the emergence of collective bargaining. Yet despite the fact that some state statutes provide that aspects of the merit system be excluded from collective bargaining, there is little convincing evidence that the merit system in the public sector is eroding because of the collective bargaining process.

Restraints on Strikes

The purpose of an economic strike in the private sector is generally to put economic pressure on the employer; if the firm is deprived of revenue, the employer may be faced with losses. The private employer has options in this situation: locking out employees, hiring replacements, or shutting down operations. Thus, there appears to be a measure of economic power on both sides. In the public sector, however, the strike is focused more on political pressure, and a government unit is not under the same economic and financial stress that a private employer may face. Nevertheless, government officials are under political pressures to eliminate the inconvenience or disruptions of the strike.

The strike is one of the basic issues that differentiates public sector and private sector labor relations. Not only is it that the strike serves different purposes in the two sectors; in most public jurisdictions, the strike is illegal. Since 1970, ten states have granted the right to strike to some public employees. But even in these states, strikes that present a threat to public health, safety, or welfare are prohibited, and essential services are protected by provision of compulsory arbitration for some groups of employees.

Despite the general prohibition of strikes, strikes have occurred and continue to occur. The situations that give rise such action are similar to those of other strikes, but the illegality of the public sector strikes often brings public condemnation and sometimes monetary penalties. Police and firefighters hesitate to call a strike because public safety is directly involved. Other government employees as well may be reluctant to strike because of the illegality of the action.

These restraints undoubtedly have had some impact on the ability of public sector unions to attain some of their goals. The substitution of fact-finding and arbitration procedures for the strike often relieves the pressures to engage in an illegal strike.

Standards or Criteria for Wage Negotiations

In the negotiations of a wage adjustment, a number of key criteria or standards are generally referred to by one or both of the parties:

1. Cost of living.
2. Pattern of settlements in the community.
3. Comparable wages in comparable communities.
4. Employer's ability to pay.
5. Productivity.
6. Equity wage adjustments.

It should be noted that no single criterion is generally fully acceptable to both parties.

Cost of Living

In many negotiations, one of the standard criteria for wage adjustments is the change in the cost of living, which one or the other of the parties may use in its arguments, depending on economic conditions. Various problems arise in applying this standard. Should one use the changes of the cost-of-living index over the previous months (that is, covering a period of the past collecting bargaining agreement)? Should one use national indexes or regional measures? Should one extrapolate the past trend for the period of the new contract? Unlike the private sector, relatively few collective bargaining agreements in the public sector contain cost-of-living adjustment clauses that automatically kick in wage adjustments on a regular prescribed basis, based on the changes in the U.S. Department of Labor's cost-of-living index. Because state and local governments have fixed budgets, changes in the cost of living are more likely to be used in bargaining as a criterion at contract time to justify a wage demand or a wage offer.

The cost of living is normally tied to the Consumer Price Index (CPI), published monthly by the U.S. Department of Labor's

Bureau of Labor Statistics (BLS). Two separate sets of data are published: one for "all urban consumers," which covers professional, managerial, and technical workers, the self-employed, short-term workers, the unemployed, retirees, and others not in the labor force, and another for "urban wage earners and clerical workers." In addition to the national data, the BLS publishes statistics regularly for fifteen selected areas. When negotiating parties discuss the issue of cost-of-living changes, which of these options should be used? Naturally, each side is likely to propose the index that is most favorable to its position.

Pattern of Settlements in the Community

Coordination among unions fluctuates over time and among communities, and it is difficult to determine whether such coordination occurs more frequently in the public or the private sector. Nevertheless, it is not uncommon for one party or the other (and sometimes both) to refer to the pattern of settlements in the community during the negotiations of a wage adjustment. In some localities, there are councils of construction trades unions, and the coordination of various labor relations activities has been successful in many communities, although these often negotiate separately. In some instances metal trades councils negotiate as a single unit and sign a single collective bargaining agreement. And in some cases the agreement is with a public employer, such as a navy yard.[3]

It is not uncommon in the public sector for the public safety unions (police and fire) to vie with each other rather than coordinate their labor relations activities. In some cases, it is a historic accident that one of the two safety unions will be the leader in settling first, with the other settling afterward, with a similar bargaining package. In some cases, one union may hold back, waiting for the other to settle first, so it can attempt to get more. Some communities make every effort to offer and settle each of its collective bargaining agreements with the identical wage adjustment. Here, one or more of the unions may attempt to break the pattern, either because it believes it deserves more than the others or perhaps because it overestimates its own power and leverage. But even where a uniform wage offer by a community is accepted by all unions, there is still flexibility in other issues on the negotiating table. Some items may involve considerable cost to the employer, while others may involve language but no money. Since relatively few collective bargaining settlements involve only a wage adjustment, comparing the total costs of one package with that of another union may be exceedingly difficult, if not impossible. Fringe items for police, firefighters, municipal employees, and teachers may vary significantly, and comparisons of costs are frequently difficult to make. In addition, there are distinctive elements to each union or service, such as detail rates, court time, and uniform allowance, that may make comparisons even more difficult.

Almost all items in a collective bargaining agreement, whether a money item or not, involve a cost to one side or the other. Once an item is included in an agreement, there is generally a direct cost in bargaining it out of the agreement. Thus, the costs of a bargaining package are difficult to calculate, and even when they are computed, it is still difficult to negotiate agreements for different unions with total costs that look identical to the different unions. Each union faces distinctive problems that are dealt with in the collective bargaining agreement, and an item of high value and cost to one union may have no value to another union.

Comparable Wages in Comparable Communities

Another criterion used by public sector unions and public managements in local communities is the comparable wage paid for the same or similar work in neighboring or in comparable communities. There is no automaticity in this criterion. Should the follower catch up with the leader, or maintain the old differential? If the answer is to close the gap with the leader, by how much and how fast? Are there special or peculiar factors that account for one community's being ahead of the others? And if so, should the higher wage be discounted? Another matter that is frequently in dispute is the identification of relevant comparable communities. Should the communities selected for comparison be only the contiguous ones or those within the radius of, say, one hundred miles? Is the size of the comparison communities to be considered? And what about the wealth, income level, and tax base of the comparable communities? In some instances, the dispute over selecting comparable communities may be just as difficult as that of determining an appropriate wage increase.

Another aspect of this criterion is a determination of the jobs or skills for which wages are to be compared. For unique skills, such as transit operators, police, and firefighters, this issue is generally not serious, although job content may vary among communities of different size. The comparison of wages with nonunion communities may be a debated issue. Where public service skills are found in the private sector (maintenance workers, custodians, truck drivers), wage comparability may become a complex matter, and the comparison of related fringe benefits can be very contentious.

Ability to Pay

In some state statutes covering collective bargaining for public sector employees, a community's ability to pay is specifically noted as a factor to be considered when determining wages for public employees. The issue that frequently arises is how to determine the community's ability to pay. What does the concept mean in the complexities of public accounting? Since the determination of budgets and priorities is a political process, how can collective bargaining influence such decisions? If an arbitrator is involved in the case, does he or she have the authority to examine the records and decide on these complexities? If there is a fixed fund for wage adjustments, will the last union making a settlement find no funds available in the community's offers? If a community decides to build a golf course and allocate its discretionary funds for construction, does this mean the community does not have the ability to pay for a wage increase for its teachers? If the community has the right and ability to raise taxes or fees but refuses to do so to fund a wage increase for its employers, has the community met the criterion of inability to pay for the wage increase? The answers to these questions vary from case to case, and rarely is there a uniform response across the nation.

The structure of funding and accounting in public sector communities makes it exceedingly difficult to determine whether a community has the ability to pay for a wage increase proposed by an employee organization.[4] Related to a community's ability to pay for a specific wage increase agreed to at the bargaining table is the structure of local taxes, which in itself has important ramifications for collective bargaining results. According to one study, cities that are successful in shifting some of the incidence of local taxes to nonresidents pay higher wages to their public employees. Cities with higher levels of family income pay higher wages to public employees. And city managers were found to raise wages and reduce employment, leaving overall payrolls unchanged.[5]

Ability to pay as a criterion for a wage adjustment is a complex matter, involving numerous items in the community: the level and incidence of taxes, the income levels of the residents, the number of employee organizations demanding wage increases, and the level of wage increases demanded. However, in collective bargaining, many other criteria may be introduced to justify or deny a wage proposal. The cost-of-living argument or the wage in comparable communities may be used, and these criteria need not come out with the same results, all favoring the position of one side or the other. The question also arises whether ability to pay is a criterion that is conclusive. An employer may well argue, particularly in good times, that its ability to pay does not necessarily justify a wage or salary increase.

Productivity

Because of the nature of products and services offered by the public sector, labor productivity often may not be readily measurable in some reasonable or acceptable manner. Consider, for example, the measurement of productivity in the school system (although class size may be considered a measure of productivity). Nevertheless, public complaints are made that rising wage and salary scales for public employees are not accompanied by commensurate improvements in services rendered with reference to such indexes of performance as school reading levels, crime rates, dirty streets, delays in processing official papers, court delays, and the like. In the same vein, unions have been accused of obstructing progress, imposing excessive staffing patterns, preventing modernization of procedures, insulating employees from scrutiny and evaluation, and tying management's hands.[6] There are, of course, some groups of public employees for whom productivity has been considered an appropriate criterion for wage adjustments, and work rules changes have led to "productivity increases."

Equity Wage Adjustments

An interesting aspect of the wage goals of unions in the public sector is their involvement in equity wage adjustments for women. Public unions have sought the implementation of the principle of what has commonly been referred to as comparable worth, which would raise the wages of jobs primarily held by women. According to one study of this issue, it is a program to achieve pay equity between women's jobs, such as nurses, and men's jobs, such as garbage collectors, where the market place pays higher wages to the garbage collectors.[7] Comparable worth is a means of arriving at the goal of pay equity—a form of job evaluation procedures that may be used to establish the relative value, and hence pay, of various job classifications for a single employer. It is "the system of compensation that is utilized once there exists a non-sex-based evaluation of all jobs within a given firm or agency."[8] Although some efforts at comparable pay have been made through collective bargaining, litigation and lobbying have also been an important part of the strategy of some labor organizations. Advocates of using comparable worth in setting pay argue that jobs of comparable value to the employer should be paid comparable wages. In job evaluation, jobs are broken down by attributes, or job factors, and the various factors are then valued. Generally the result of such a technique has been to raise the pay in clerical occupations and certain professions (such as nursing) relative to blue-collar occupations.[9] These internal wage relations depart from exterior or market wage relationships that are said to be sex biased.

The question of low pay for women in specific occupations was first made into a significant issue under the Equal Pay Act of 1963, which outlawed separate pay scales for men and women using similar skills and performing work under the same conditions. The lower-paying jobs in clerical work and nursing classifications are highly dominated by women, and there are few, if any, men's jobs with which they could be appropriately compared in the same agency. Courts dealing with this issue consistently refused to consider the comparison of female jobs with dissimilar work done by males, on the grounds that this was ruled out by the Equal Pay Act. Nevertheless, court challenges to pay inequities did provide significant impetus for implementation of comparable worth in the early 1980s. In 1983 AFSCME filed a case against Washington State that took the step of comparing worth of different jobs. The union's case was based on job evaluation studies carried out first in 1974 by the state and updated biennially thereafter, for a total of five separate studies. Each job evaluation study showed that jobs in which women dominated (70 percent or more) were consistently underpaid at an average of about 20 percent when compared to jobs in male-dominated titles. The district court held that the state knowingly discriminated against its employees and directed the state to implement a system of payment based on comparable worth to eliminate these discrepancies. AFSCME and other unions filed similar cases elsewhere. Studies were initiated in various places through collective bargaining, and several states and local communities have adopted legislation mandating the institution of comparable worth systems of payment for their employees.[10]

It is clear that a number of factors sharply distinguish labor relations in the public and private sectors. While some factors seem to put the government employees at a disadvantage compared to private sector employees, all told, government employees appear to do as well as their counterparts in the private sector. The same sets of standards or criteria are used for wage adjustments in both sectors, although their applicability may vary between the two sectors; and even in the same sector there may be substantial variation.

Questions for Discussion

1. Why is the right of workers to organize into unions more limited in the public sector than in the private sector? Is there such a basic difference that the rights of government employees should be more restrictive? Is there a rationale for having each state with its own legislation? Why should federal, state, and local employees be treated differently?

2. Is the civil service merit system an acceptable rationale for limiting the scope of collective bargaining in the public sector? How do you explain why the civil servant cannot bargain over wages while government employees such as naval shipyard

workers, police officers and teachers have the right to bargain over wages?

3. How do you explain the fact that in recent years many public sector bargaining units have made wage gains in excess of gains made in the private sector? Have the restraints on strikes had an effect on wage bargaining in the public sector? What are the alternatives to strikes that public unions have used? Have arguments such as productivity or ability to pay been persuasive in the public sector?

4. Do you feel that the "wage equity" thrust of some unions to obtain higher wages for women's occupations will be successful? Why or why not? Is it equitable for a school custodian (male) to earn more than a school teacher (female)? How would you explain such a differential?

Case 1: An Amicable Settlement

The city of Marlwood and the Marlwood Municipal Employees Association have engaged in collective bargaining for twelve years. Over the years, the bargaining representatives have been the same persons on both sides—the same mayor and the same bargaining committee of the union—and the agreements generally have been negotiated with very little rancor or animosity. Each agreement was a three-year contract. Unions of the city's three other bargaining units consistently began their negotiations with the city after the settlement by the Municipal Employees Association, and with slight variations they followed the wage pattern set by that association.

As had been customary, the parties began contract negotiations in early April, three months before the expiration of their current agreement. The economy had taken a downturn in the fall of the previous year, with the region especially hard hit; two major industrial plants in the city had shut down just prior to Christmas. A short time before the start of the negotiations, the city announced it was having financial difficulties, and it was concerned about the deepening recession.

At the first bargaining session, the mayor, as representative of the city's negotiating team (which included three members of the city council), and the union president, spokesman of his negotiating team, spoke amicably about the national and regional recession and how each felt the city would be affected. They then presented their respective offers and demands. Much to the surprise of both parties, they were much further apart on the wage increase than ever before, although the other issues put on the table seemed minor. The union was proposing an across-the-board wage increase of 7 percent in each year of the three-year contract. The city was proposing a wage adjustment of 3 percent at the start of a one-year agreement.

After four bargaining sessions over six weeks, the union lowered its wage demand to 6.5 percent for each of the three years. The city agreed to some of the union's nonwage proposals but stuck to its proposed 3 percent increase in a one-year contract. The parties knew that if they could reach an agreement on the wage adjustment, the other issues could easily be wrapped up.

The union used these principal arguments to support its wage proposal:

1. Although its wage increase in the previous agreement was 5.5 percent per year, the cost of living had been rising by close to 6.5 percent, and it was necessary to catch up in lost real income.
2. Wage settlements over the past year in the communities the union considered comparable ranged from 6 percent to 7 percent, and it was equitable for the union to obtain a 6.5 percent increase.
3. The city did have the ability to pay the wage increase proposed by the union. The city had significant amounts of money coming in from various sources, and the tax rate was unchanged for three years.
4. In reference to a three-year contract, the union argued that each of the previous four settlements was to extend for three years and this created stable labor relations without constant negotiations and frictions.

The city, for its part, advanced these points:

1. Due to the economic conditions in the nation and the region, the cost of living was rising at an annual rate of only 4 percent, and most economic forecasts indicated a further decline in the cost-of-living index over the next twelve months.

2. Recent wage settlements for the forthcoming one-year period in communities the city considered comparable ranged from 2.5 to 3.5 percent. Even if city employees received no wage increase, their wage levels would continue to be higher than those in the comparable communities.

3. The city's ability to pay any wage increase was seriously damaged by the recession, and the economic situation looked bleak. The city noted that it had three other bargaining units to deal with, and that any wage settlement made with the Municipal Employees Association would have to be offered to the others because of the long history of parity in wage adjustments.

4. In view of the uncertainty of the general economic climate and the city's ability to pay in the future, a one-year agreement could be financed. If the city's situation improved over the year, a second one-year contract could improve the wage adjustment.

Six more bargaining sessions were held over the next three months (nearly six weeks into the new contract year) before the parties reached agreement on a wage adjustment and on the duration of the contract. The additional issues, all of them minor, were quickly settled, and the agreement was signed. The agreement was taken to a special union meeting and ratified by a substantial majority of the membership. The mayor took the agreement to the city council for funding, and it was unanimously approved. The employees of this bargaining unit received their retroactive wage adjustments, and the city began serious negotiations with the unions of the three other bargaining units.

Discussion Issues, Problems, and Questions

1. Both parties used the cost-of-living argument to support its proposals. If you look at actual CPI figures, you are looking at what has happened in the past. A union-management agreement is for the future, and projected cost-of-living changes are best guesses by experts, who may vary by a number of percentage points. Are past figures or projected figures preferable in the case involving Marlwood and its Municipal Employees Association? Why?

2. Both parties apparently agree that what other communities are doing should be given some weight in the settlement in Marl-

wood. The union selected as comparables other cities within a radius of seventy-five miles. The city selected as comparable those communities (none of which were cities) that were contiguous or near contiguous with Marlwood. Which of these choices is correct? Do you need more information about the comparables, such as population size, average income level, property tax base, or timing of the wage adjustments? How would such information help resolve the selection of comparable communities? Are there right and wrong answers in the selection of comparables?

Even if the parties were to agree on comparable communities, it is clear that the concern should be limited to the amount of wage adjustment and the timing of the adjustment. Do you take into account the granting of fringe benefits, such as longer vacations, additional holidays, or personal days? If so, how are the costs of these fringes to be calculated?

Marlwood made the argument that the relative standing of the level of wages of Marlwood employees among the comparable communities would not change even if Marlwood employees received no increase. How much weight should one give to such an argument? Is this argument more or less important than the wage adjustments made by the comparable communities?

3. Can one accurately determine whether a community has the ability to pay a wage increase proposed by a union? If a bargaining unit of, say, five employees asks for a 20 percent wage increase at the start of a community's fiscal year before any other financial commitments were made, would the community have the ability to pay for it? However, if the bargaining unit contained two thousand employees and it was the end of the fiscal year, would the community's ability to pay look different? What happens if a community has the ability to pay the wage demand of the first bargaining unit entering negotiation but will not have the ability to pay anything to the last bargaining unit in negotiation?

4. How significant is the duration of the contract? Which party gains by a longer duration of a contract? Does the provision for a wage reopener some time after the first year of a multiple-year contract resolve the issue of contract duration?

5. In view of all the considerations and arguments, what would you

propose as a fair and equitable resolution of the contract negotiations between Marlwood and the Marlwood Municipal Employees Association?

Case 2: Personalities Affecting a Settlement

The town of Darwell and the Municipal Police Association have engaged in collective bargaining for about twenty years. Over the past eight years, the town manager has been the negotiator for the town, and the union president has negotiated for the union. There was a personality conflict between the two spokesmen from the start, and this animosity affected all bargaining, with each negotiation bitter, acrimonious, and drawn out, even after the other four bargaining units in the town had reached rather speedy and satisfactory contracts.

The current two-year contract with the police officers was due to expire on June 30. Proper notice was given by the union to the town manager, and the first joint meeting to negotiate a new contract was held on March 15. The other four bargaining units, with contracts expiring on the same date, had held their first negotiation session with the town manager prior to March 15.

At the first session between the town and the police union, both sides took extreme positions. The town manager offered no increase in each of two years and the right of the police chief to reassign shifts, disregarding seniority; the union proposed a 7.5 percent increase in wages in each of the two years, a $2.00 per hour increase in the detail rate,[11] and an extra week's vacation after five years of service. The meeting was brief, and no date was set for a second negotiation session.

The town manager continued to hold bargaining sessions with the other bargaining units, and prior to July 1, each had settled for a 5.5 percent increase in each of two years, with no other changes. The town manager recommended funding of these collective bargaining agreements, and the town meeting voted approval. The employees in these bargaining units began receiving their higher wages effective July 1. The police union held its second negotiation meeting with the town manager in mid-July, with both sides fully aware of the identical settlement made by the other bargaining units.

Little was accomplished at this second meeting, and negotiations dragged on into the fall. With no right to strike, there were a number of instances of the "blue flu," with large numbers of police officers calling in sick, and some town officials began receiving questionable parking violation tickets. The town manager reacted by indicating that the police might lose all retroactivity if and when an agreement was reached. Both parties refused the services of a state mediator.

The union supported its demands by indicating that it would take a 7.5 percent increase to bring its wage levels to those of its three contiguous communities and that the other items proposed would bring the Darwell police in line with the police of the neighboring communities. The town manager argued that the wages of the police were already in line with those of police of comparable size and industrial structure (not the larger cities contiguous to Darwell), and the right to reassign shifts was important for the police chief's efficient use of his officers.

At the eleventh session, in early December, the union offered to accept the 5.5 percent settlement of the other bargaining units and to drop its other demands. The town manager agreed to the wage adjustment but insisted the police chief needed the right to reassign shifts. The union balked, and an agreement was not reached. The following day, the local newspaper detailed the final bargaining positions of the parties and then quoted the town manager and the police chief as indicating the vital importance to the efficiency and effectiveness of the police department of the right to reassign shifts. A few days later, the police chief was interviewed on a local radio station and stated he needed the right to reassign shifts in order to run the police department. The local press and ration supported the police chief.

At the next negotiation session, the union, realizing that it had lost public support over the issue of the police chief's right to reassign shifts, agreed to accept the last offer of the town. The union knew it needed public support at town meeting to have its wage increase funded. The agreement was signed and submitted to the next town meeting for funding. By a narrow margin, the town meeting refused to fund the agreement, sending the parties back to the bargaining table.

Discussion Issues, Problems, and Questions

1. In previous negotiations, the identical wage adjustment was offered to each of the five bargaining units and the wage settlements were always identical. There were often other demands that were unique to any one group, and they occasionally were granted by the town. In the current set of negotiations, the four units (other than the police) settled for only a wage increase; no other matters were included in the settlement. Was the town's insistence that the police chief be given the right to reassign shifts a real need or the result of the animosity between the town manager and the union president? Since the police chief in none of the comparable communities had such a right, how would you explain the Darwell situation? If you were a consultant to the union at the very early stages of the negotiations, what would you have advised the union to do? Would you have suggested a change in the composition of the union negotiating team?

2. Why did both the union and the town reject the offer of mediation? Did the union feel it could do better than the other bargaining units if there were no outside mediator in the picture? Or was it a matter of personal pride of the union president?

3. The union knew it would need general public support for any agreement reached. Do you feel the union supported the idea of a blue flu and giving out questionable parking tickets to town officials? How could the union offset the bad publicity it got from the police chief's going public on the issue of the right to reassign shifts?

4. Once the town meeting refused to fund the package, what were the union's options?

Case 3: Union Political Action

The town of Dorton and the four bargaining units of the town employees had had reasonably good labor relations for quite a number of years. The general municipal employees were the first to organize shortly after the three largest private employers of the town signed collective bargaining agreements with the same union. These private employers signed up with the union after a moderately long strike that had the overwhelming open support of the town's voters. The town officials—the mayor and the town select-men—were more cautious in indicating their position on the strike, and some groups of townspeople were critical of these officials. Nevertheless, when the strike was over and the union signed agreements with the three private companies calling for substantial wage increases, all bitterness and rancor seemed to fade. Shortly after the general municipal employees, with the support of the private sector union, organized a union, which was promptly recognized by the town officials. After a few negotiation sessions, again with the assistance of the private sector union, a satisfactory collective bargaining agreement was signed.

Less than a year after the general municipal employees signed their contract with the town, the firefighters formed a union and asked for recognition. The town officials balked. They viewed firefighters as in a unique category and saw no need for the firefighters to organize. Nevertheless, all the firefighters joined the newly formed union, and the town began negotiations. After a number of long and hard sessions, the first contract was signed, giving the firefighters sufficient benefits to be pleased.

Within six months after the firefighters signed their contract, the teachers and the police officers formed unions, negotiated with the town officials, and signed contracts. In both cases the negotiations went smoothly and quickly, and the wage gains largely followed the increases received by the firefighters.

Soon after these collective bargaining agreements were signed, town elections were held. As was traditional, there was no recognized opposition for the town officials, all of whom ran for reelection. In the few instances where there was opposition, the city official running for reelection won the race. The reelected town officials then negotiated new contracts with each of the bargaining units. Each package differed slightly and each unit gained some noncost items, but the wage adjustment in percentage was identical in all four agreements. The town did succeed in adjusting the duration of each contract so that all expired on the same date.

At the next election, a group of younger citizens who had been very active in support of strike in the private sector a few years back organized to put a slate in opposition to the office holders, all of whom were running for reelection. Town elections in the past had hardly raised a flutter, and incumbents who ran for reelection almost always won. The opposition group, with the support of private sector union workers, ran a well-organized campaign. Nevertheless, there appeared to be relatively limited interest in the election. The incumbents were confident, and the general public apparently assumed that, as in the past, the incumbents would win. When campaign literature noted that these incumbents were the same town officials who had not openly supported the strike against the three large private firms in the town, the firefighters' union came out in support of the opposition group. The three other public sector unions did not actively support either side in the election. Much to the surprise of many citizens, the opposition group defeated all the incumbents by a slight majority. For the first time in the town's election history, all of the town's elected officials were swept out of office in a single election.

A few months after the election, the new mayor and his team began negotiating with each public sector union over new contracts. Each union had developed its own package of demands, and the wage adjustments proposed ranged from 6 to 8.5 percent. The town offered a uniform wage adjustment of 3 percent to all unions and indicated a willingness to consider some nonwage benefits. After a number of bargaining sessions with each union, agreements were reached with the general municipal workers, the teachers, and the police for a 4 percent across-the-board wage increase in each of the two years of the agreement, plus additional fringe benefits at the start of the first year, which amounted to about another 1 percent. Some noncost items were also agreed to in each of the three agreements.

The firefighters held out for more. They demanded a 5 percent general wage increase in each of two years plus fringe benefits amounting to about 3 percent. The union's justification was the situation of firefighters in comparable communities. The town negotiator noted that the other unions had made similar legitimate comparisons but still settled for less because of the town's economic situation compared to the comparable communities.

Neither party officially spoke to the local press about the ongoing negotiations, but the press was curious about why the firefighters were still negotiating after the other three unions had settled in the same monetary package. Someone then leaked the information on the union's demands to the press, and the paper editorialized whether the union was seeking payment for its political support in the elections. At the next negotiation session, the parties struck an agreement of a 4.5 percent across-the-board increase in each of the two years of the contract and a fringe package deal estimated to cost approximately 2 percent. This agreement was presented to the next meeting of the board of selectmen for funding and was unanimously approved.

Discussion Issues, Problems, and Questions

1. The facts are clear that the firefighters' union negotiated better terms in its contract than did the other three public sector unions. The firefighters got a 0.5 percent larger wage increase and a 1 percent larger fringe benefit package than did the other unions. There was no proof that the firefighters union was paid off by the mayor and the selectmen for the political support in the previous town election. The evidence was circumstantial. Do you think it was a payoff? Why?

2. The firefighters' union presented strong evidence that its demands were in line with firefighter settlements in comparable communities. The town negotiators did not argue that the evidence was wrong or that the union had selected wrong communities as comparables. The town acknowledged the correctness of the union agreement but argued it could not afford to pay more than what it agreed to pay to the other unions. Perhaps the union realized the town did have enough funds to pay it more. If so, was it wrong for the union to try to get more for its members than the other unions got? What ethical standards should we use to make this judgment?

3. Is it possible that the negotiators for the firefighters' union were more skilled at negotiating than were the negotiators of the other unions? Were the firefighters' negotiators more capable than the town negotiators? Is it more important to have the basic economic factors on your side or to have the more skilled and capable negotiator?

4. Could the bargaining results that occurred in this town with the four unions have occurred in the private sector? Why or why not?

5. In view of what happened in Dorton, and in order to avoid the

semblance of a payoff, should public sector unions be prohibited from participating in the political arena?

Case 4: Need for City Council Support

The city of Hartshorne had been negotiating with seven different unions representing workers in seven bargaining units for more than twenty years. From the start, the city had hired a large law firm to do all of its labor relations work, and this law firm still represented the city in all of its labor relations with the unions. Over the years, six of the seven unions hired attorneys to deal with the city in all labor relations matters—a move largely to offset the apparent advantage the city had with its law firm, which specialized in labor law for management. The one union that did not employ an attorney to represent it in contract negotiations or in grievance arbitration was the Public Works Employees Association. The president of this union was one of the organizers when it was first formed, and he had represented this union in all contract negotiations and arbitrations.

Over the years, the parties apparently found it more convenient not to have all seven collective bargaining agreements terminate on the same date. Except for the unions representing the police officers and the firefighters, there was relatively little attempt at pattern bargaining within the city or a follow-the-leader pattern, where the settlement with one union paved the way for all the others. The police union and the firefighters' union did compete with each other, and each tried to make sure the other did not get a better deal.

At the start of the current round of contract negotiations the city was facing a downturn in its economy, with an unemployment rate of 6.5 percent. Local economists were forecasting a rise in the unemployment rate to somewhat over 7 percent in the next twelve months. Recent wage settlements in the private sector of the city ranged from 3 to 4 percent. In a press conference the mayor indicated the city was facing a financial crunch and might have to lay off some city employees.

Within the first six months of the round of contract negotiations, four of the unions (except the police, fire, and public works) reached agreements with the city, with the settlements ranging from 3.5 to 4.5 percent in wage adjustments and from 0 to 1 percent in fringes. The mayor estimated that the costs of the total contract packages ranged from 3.5 to 5 percent, and he indicated the city might lay off some of the public employees to offset the costs of the settlements.

The police were next to settle, gaining a wage adjustment of 5 percent and fringe benefits valued at 0.5 percent. The local press and radio and television stations editorialized about the "greediness" of the police when the city was hard pressed financially and unemployment was spreading. This outburst of public protest seemed to put a damper on the firefighters' negotiations, and the union found it convenient not to schedule negotiation sessions too soon afterward. About two months after the police settlement, the firefighters reached an agreement with the city for a 4.5 percent wage increase and changes in some fringe benefits. The parties sidestepped the question of the value of the fringe benefit changes, and this settlement received very little publicity.

The public works employees were still without a contract and were still meeting with city representatives regularly to negotiate. At the session shortly after the firefighters' settlement, the union president indicated that his staff estimated the cost of the firefighters' fringe benefits at 1 percent, making a package of 5.5 percent, equal to that of the police. The city representatives and their legal spokesman refused to discuss the estimate. The union aggressively continued to push for its demands for a 5 percent wage increase and fringe benefits valued at 2 percent. The city was offering a 4 percent wage adjustment and no fringe benefit changes. After further discussion of the firefighters' settlement, the parties seemed to be willing to consider some change in positions and agreed to another session in two weeks.

Before negotiations had started between the city and the public works union, the union had filed a grievance against the city, contending an ongoing violation of an overtime provision of the collective bargaining agreement. The grievance went to arbitration, and the day following the negotiation session when the firefighters' fringe benefit gains were discussed, the arbitrator handed down his award. The award upheld the grievance and ordered the city to pay the union $17,000 back pay of unpaid overtime. The award was taken to the city council that week for funding and was unanimously rejected.

The union went into the next bargaining session with great trepidation. Prior to the city council's refusal to fund the arbitration award, the union president thought he had an excellent chance of reaching a settlement in excess of 5.5 percent. He undoubtedly realized that any settlement that looked excessive would be rejected by the city council, forcing the parties back to the bargaining table. The city attorney came into the session without a change in its position: a 4 percent wage adjustment and no changes in fringe benefits. He informed the union negotiators that the mayor could recommend this package to the city council and that the council would likely approve it. The union negotiators went out to caucus and after an hour returned and indicated they would accept the offer.

The following week, the union negotiating team brought the agreement to a union membership meeting for ratification. The union president explained the reasons for accepting the package offered by the city and put his prestige on the line in recommending its ratification. The negotiating team unanimously supported the president's position. By a slight majority, the union voted to ratify the agreement. Two weeks later, the city council funded the agreement by a unanimous vote.

Discussion Issues, Problems, and Questions

1. The Hartshorne Public Works Employees' Association was the only union in the public sector that had not hired a labor attorney to deal with the city and its attorney. The union president, who was a leader in the formation of the union and had been the chief negotiator and spokesman ever since, learned his skills on the job and had been a reasonably effective spokesman for the union. Over the years, would the union have been more successful at the bargaining table had it hired an attorney to deal with the city? Would the union have lost a personal relationship with the mayor had the union president been replaced as a spokesman by a lawyer? In your judgment, how significant are personal relationships in the collective bargaining area?

2. In most organized private enterprises, management deals with a single (and occasionally a second) labor organization. In the public sector, it would be relatively unusual if management dealt with fewer than three unions. In many moderately sized cities where the public service employees have organized, management may be dealing with six to ten labor organizations. Is this an advantage or disadvantage for any one of the numerous unions negotiating with the same employer? If management of a community has a relatively fixed sum for wage increases, how is the money to be given out? Is the last union to negotiate at a disadvantage? Should management make every effort to have all contracts expire on the same date, thereby not giving an advantage to any single union?

3. If a city council has the right to refuse to fund a tentative agreement reached by a mayor and a union, what options does the union have? If the parties must go back to the negotiation table to start anew, the odds are that the union will get less than it had originally settled for. Is such a system fair and equitable? What is the rationale of giving the legislative body the authority to refuse to fund a wage agreement? Why not permit the union to strike over such a decision?

4. In the Hartshorne case, the city council's decision on the grievance award made it clear to the union what it would likely do on a wage agreement that exceeded some norm. Should the union have taken the chance and continued to battle for a higher wage package? If the union could have gotten more at the negotiation table, could it have won at the city council? Is lobbying and the ballot box the only real long-run solution for public sector unions?

4

Monetary Fringe Benefits

In the private sector, there are few terms and conditions of employment that are outside the scope of collective bargaining. Once a bargaining unit is determined, the employee organization representing the workers in that unit has broad rights to bargain with the employer over wages, hours, and other conditions of employment for those workers. The meanings of these words have broadened over time, and there is little that affects bargaining unit workers that has been specifically excluded from the scope of bargaining. Certain issues have been classified as mandatory topics for negotiations: wages, benefits, hours, holidays, vacations, working rules, and grievance procedures. Illegal topics for negotiations would cover matters whose inclusion in a labor contract would violate some public policy. All other issues are called permissive topics; the parties are not obliged to negotiate on these subjects, but they may choose to do so.

In the public sector, the scope of bargaining is much more limited, generally by statute. For federal agencies and employees who are covered by the Federal Service Labor Management Relations Statute, the scope of the duty to bargain includes personnel policies, practices, and matters affecting working conditions to the extent not inconsistent with federal law, or government-wide rules or regulations, or an agency rule or regulation for which a "compelling need" exists. The duty to bargain does not extend to policies, practices, or matters relating to certain prohibited political activities, the classification of any position, or matters specifically provided for by federal statute. Bargaining is generally not permitted on wages and fringe benefits. In addition, the duty to bargain is further limited by a statutory management rights section that is broader and more rigid than such clauses found in private sector agreements.[1]

Federal employees are thus allowed to bargain on the numbers, types, and grades of employee, work methods and technology, the procedures for exercising managerial authority, and the rights of employees adversely affected by this authority. Grievance and arbitration procedures are an intrinsic part of the negotiations and required in all collective bargaining agreements in the federal sector. Monetary fringe benefits for federal employees are not within the permissible scope of collective bargaining because they are determined by legislation.

Unlike the federal sector, most monetary fringe benefits are within the scope of bargaining for state and local employees. There is substantial variation in the specific coverage among the states, but most states require bargaining over wages, hours, and the significant conditions of employment. How such words are interpreted varies substantially among state laws, state employment relations boards, and state courts. Nevertheless, most of the typically negotiated monetary fringe benefits are found, in varying degrees and among various groups, in collective bargaining agreements involving state and local employees. Certain fringe benefits are a normal part of the negotiations in the private sector but are generally excluded from public sector bargaining. These include health benefits but not the relative shares of the employer and the worker, workers' compensation insurance, unemployment insurance, and retirement benefits—all of which are normally provided by federal or state statute and cover all public employees.

In the private sector, basically all nonexempt employees are covered by the same federal relations laws and rules; only a few special groups of workers, such as employees involved basically in intrastate commerce, are carved out for different treatment in negotiations with employers.[2] In the public sector, however, most states and localities have different laws and rules for their uniformed employees (police and fire), and frequently schoolteachers are treated differently. As a result, there may be significant variations among different employee groups in the use of certain monetary fringe benefits, as well as nonmonetary benefits. Considerable variations in benefits also exist not because of the imposition of outside laws or rules but because of the nature of the job itself. Teachers, for example, who normally have the summer off, surely view vacations differently than do police, firefighters, or clerical workers in city hall. Uniform or uniform cleaning allowances are viewed differently by police and firefighters than by teachers. The significance of an overtime benefit may vary greatly between a police officer and a town clerk.

Nonwage Benefits

The fact that a union may negotiate long and hard for what it considers an important benefit and may be prepared to trade off part of a wage adjustment does not necessarily mean there is a direct money value to that benefit. To some groups of employees, there are nonmonetary benefits that may far outweigh the significance of a monetary fringe—for example, the scope of the grievance procedure, a union security provision, dues checkoff, the number of firefighters on a piece of equipment, the number of officers in a police car, or the size of classes for teachers. Nevertheless, many of these nonmonetary items may involve a direct or administrative cost to the employer. Thus, the fact that an item in negotiations is labeled a monetary or a nonmonetary benefit does not automatically indicate its importance. Each bargaining unit may give a different weight to a specific fringe item because of the nature of the job or the profession. And within a single bargaining unit, different groups may have varying priorities among benefits depending on such factors as age, seniority, and education. An older group, for example, may give a higher priority to a pension benefit than to an immediate wage increase. A younger group, on the other hand, which accepts and performs the vast majority of overtime work, would give a higher priority to an increase in overtime opportunities than to some other fringe benefits.

In the private sector, a number of so-called standard or common monetary fringes are found in most collective bargaining agreements and in many nonunion firms as part of their personnel policies: overtime rates and policies, holidays and holiday pay, conditions for vacations and amount of vacation, shift differentials, reporting and callback pay, sick leave, personal leave, group health and life insurance, and pensions. The level of benefits of these items may vary substantially from firm to firm, industry to industry, location to location, by size of firm, and by profitability of the firm.

In the public sector, many of these fringes are provided by statute or regulation and are not within the collective bargaining scope. Most federal employees are covered by a uniform group insurance and pension program, as well as vacation (annual leave) and sick-leave programs. While not at the same levels as federal employees, state and local government employees are generally covered for these same fringes by state law, thereby providing uniformity for state government. The level of these benefits may vary significantly among the states and even among occupational groups within any one state. Because of the dangerous nature of their work, police officers and firefighters may have more generous group insurance and sick leave programs than other state and local government employees. Because of the nature of teachers' yearly work schedule, the conventional vacation provision does not apply to teachers.

Scope in the Federal Sector

In the federal sector, different government agencies may negotiate agreements containing slightly different monetary fringes. In reference to holidays, for example, the agreement between the U.S. Customs Service and the National Treasury Employees Union designates eleven specific holidays "for purposes of pay and leave," plus "any other day designated as a holiday by Federal Statute or Executive Order."[3] The holiday provision of the collective bargaining agreement between the Portsmouth Naval Shipyard and the Federal Employees Metal Trades Council, AFL-CIO, provides that "all employees . . . shall be entitled to all holiday benefits, which are now or in the future, granted in accordance with applicable regulations."[4] Classified federal civil service employee have a standard uniform holiday provision throughout the various federal government agencies. Because the labor relations of the Postal Service falls under the National Labor Relations Act, the federal law covering the private sector, the scope of bargaining is that permitted in the private sector.

Scope for State Employees

Many states define the scope of public employee bargaining as "wages, hours, and other terms and conditions of employment." Some states specifically exclude certain topics, such as merit pay policies and retirement benefits, while others specify each item that may be negotiated.[5] There is considerable variation in wording among the state statutes, and in a number of states there is also variation among different employee groups within the same state. In Delaware, for example, the scope of bargaining for state, county, and local employees is "wages, salaries, hours, vacations, sick leave, grievance procedures, and other terms and conditions of employment"; for teachers, the scope is "wages, salaries, hours, grievance procedures, and working conditions"; and for transit employees, the scope is "wages, salaries, hours, working conditions, health benefits, pensions, and retirement allowances."[6] Hawaii, on the other hand, does not differentiate among its various groups of public employees but describes in detail the exclusions from the scope of bargaining for all public employees:

> Wages, hours, and other terms and conditions of employment; excluding classification and reclassification, retirement, salary ranges and number of incremented and longevity steps, matters inconsistent with merit principles and equal pay for equal work principle, or managerial discipline and control.[7]

Iowa has one comprehensive public employee bargaining statute, and its scope of bargaining covers the following:

> Wages, hours, vacations, insurance, holidays, leave, shift differential, overtime, supplemental pay, seniority, transfer procedures, job classifications, health and safety evaluation, staff reduction, in-service training, and other mutually agreed upon matters; excluding merit system and retirement.[8]

In New Mexico, state employees in the classified service are covered for collective bargaining purposes by rules and regulations adopted by the State Personnel Board. The scope of bargaining for these employees is limited to terms and conditions of employment; salaries, as well as matters of classification, reclassification, and retirement benefits, are excluded.[9] In Oklahoma there are two public employee bargaining laws, one covering police and firefighters and the other covering public school employees.[10] The scope for the former reads as follows: "Wages, salaries, hours, rates of pay, grievances, working conditions and all other terms and conditions of employment." The scope for public school employees reads as follows: "Professional employees—items affecting the performance of professional services; non-professional employees—terms and conditions of employment."

Tennessee also has two public employee bargaining statutes, and they cover only teachers and transit employees.[11] The scope of bargaining for the teachers clearly specifies the numerous exclusions:

> Salaries or wages, grievance procedures, insurance, fringe benefits (excluding pensions or retirement), working conditions, leave, student discipline procedure, payroll deductions; cannot violate federal or state laws or municipal charters, employee rights, or board of education rights.

The scope of bargaining for the Tennessee transit employees contains no exclusions; it covers wages, salaries, hours, working conditions, health benefits, pensions, and retirement allowances.

In the vast majority of negotiations over monetary fringe benefits, there are considerable similarities between the private sector and state and municipal employees, with a significant exception: employees in the private sector generally have the legal right to strike. Although priorities may differ between the public and private sectors over the same fringe items (holidays, for example), these differences may be no greater than the differences among bargaining units in the private sector. Where the bargaining process over a monetary fringe and the results are not significantly different between private sector and public sector units, there seems to be little value in discussing these factors here. The purpose of this book is to point up the differences between the private and the public sector labor relations, and we will discuss here those monetary fringe items where the difference in negotiating procedures and results are significant.

In a number of jurisdictions, certain fringe items are excluded from the scope of bargaining. They are mandated by statute or administrative decision, and neither public service employees nor their representatives have bargaining rights over them. Nevertheless, the employee and the union are not without some leverage to affect the benefit. Lobbying at the state legislature or with the town's administration may be more effective than a private sector union bargaining with an industrial enterprise.

For many groups of public service employees across political jurisdictions, a number of monetary fringe items are basically similar to those commonly found in private sector collective bargaining agreements: typically overtime provisions, shift differentials, holiday pay, call-in pay, and reporting pay. For some public sector groups, such as firefighters, for example, shift differentials are not very common, principally because of their work schedule. On the other hand, school custodians, maintenance workers, and transit workers, for example, may negotiate shift differentials very similar, if not identical, to those found in the private sector.

Fringe Benefits for Special Groups

Police and firefighters have special fringes because of the nature of their jobs. Police department employees may be required to appear in court to testify on matters related to their regular duties, and so many police collective bargaining agreements contain provisions covering such court appearances. If the appearance occurs during duty hours, employees receive their regular pay; if police officers have to appear during off-duty hours, they are eligible for call-in pay, standby pay, overtime, a flat sum, or compensatory time, as specified. An off-duty appearance could compensate the officer at time and one-half the hourly rate for a minimum of five hours. This is not a common benefit for firefighters; nevertheless, some firefighters' bargaining agreements provide for court time premiums.[12]

In many collective bargaining agreements, police officers and firefighters are given extra pay for work performed under a variety of special circumstances or hazardous conditions beyond normal conditions. When special skills are required, the employees are frequently paid extra. This could apply to motorcycle officers, helicopter pilots, divers, and bomb squad work, and in some instances, skill with firearms could result in a bonus. Firefighters in a growing number of communities drive emergency ambulances and are required to be emergency medical technicians (EMTs). Contracts normally provide an annual bonus for firefighters who are EMTs and frequently provide extra payments to those who take refresher EMT courses. Because of the nature of firefighting, a number of communities prefer that all firefighters become EMTs, and this becomes a prerequisite for being employed as a firefighter. (The first case study in this chapter addresses this issue.)

In the private sector, an employee's wage or salary is based on the job rate or job rate range; a few public sector employee groups have negotiated specific wage schedules based on length of service on the job. Groups such as public school teachers, police, and firefighters, whose job promotion opportunities are very limited and whose experience is a very important factor in performance, have negotiated some form of length-of-service salary schedule. Teachers generally negotiate a salary schedule that contains ten to fifteen steps, with each step representing a year of teaching experience. Each step specifies a specific dollar salary, and the steps apply to teachers in the system and those who are hired into it with years of teaching experience in other jurisdictions. Generally, when a new contract is negotiated and a general wage increase is agreed upon, the increase is applied to all the steps in the schedule.

Police and firefighters, who normally remain at their hired-in position for a lengthy period of time before promotional opportunities occur, have developed a different form of extra pay for years of service; they receive longevity pay or a continuous-service bonus. Regardless of the name, the general practice is to provide a bonus in dollar amounts or as a percentage of annual salary to employees with a specified number of continuous years of full-time service. A common form of such a provision designates the amount of bonus after five years, ten years, fifteen years, and sometimes twenty years of service. Such bonuses are frequently adjusted when contracts are renegotiated, and occasionally the years of service required to obtain such bonuses are renegotiated.

Teachers, police, and firefighters have also negotiated some form of extra pay for additional education. Teachers have recognized this type of benefit for many years, and it is fairly common for a teachers' collective bargaining agreement to contain a salary schedule that provides a schedule with annual step increases for various levels of education, such as bachelor's degree, bachelor's degree plus thirty credits, master's degree, master's degree plus thirty credits, and doctorate. Thus, it is possible for a teacher not only to move to a higher salary step because of longevity but also to move at the same time to a higher salary level because of completion of additional education.

There has been some recognition of the importance of more education for protective service personnel. College graduates are being more actively recruited by police and fire departments, and as a result a substantial number of their collective bargaining agreements contain some form of education incentive. To encourage employees to obtain additional education and training through professionally related courses, agreements provide for educational incentive pay. These provisions call for pay differentials in accordance with the number of courses or course credits taken or the degree attained. Incentive clauses generally provide an annual stipend for attaining a certain level of education, measured by credits, courses, or degrees, but the variations in hours and educational levels are wide. Some contracts pay a dollar bonus per credit; others start at thirty credits. Some pay off at an associate's degree level and others at the bachelor's level. Some contracts pay extra for a master's degree and still more for a juris doctor degree. There have been disputes in various jurisdictions not only over the levels of educational incentives but over what is relevant education. Does the course of study have to be approved in advance, and by whom? Must the study program be limited, for example, to law enforcement? (The second case study concerns problems arising over educational incentives.)

In some instances, books and tuition aid for employees are provided by the employer, and in some cases these benefits are provided only if the employee achieves a passing grade in the course or program. In some jurisdictions, the employer pays incidental expenses incurred as a result of attending school, and in some the employee is reimbursed mileage expenses.

In addition to educational incentives, many police and fire departments require their employees to undergo inservice training programs designed to improve their professional skills and many collective bargaining agreements deal with some aspects of such job-related training—for example, the type of training, the number of hours of required training, pay guarantees for class attendance, and travel expenses. Some agreements include requirements that new employees participate in state-operated training programs.[13]

A significant majority of police and firefighter collective bargaining agreements require that the employer provide employees with uniforms or maintenance of uniforms, or both. Uniform allowance provisions typically specify the amount of the payment and often differentiate between the amount of money allocated for the purchase of clothing and for their cleaning and maintenance. The sums stipulated are generally on an annual basis. In one case, an annual new clothing allowance of $900 was granted. In some jurisdictions, repair or replacement cost of uniforms damaged in the line of duty is reimbursed to the employee; in other jurisdictions, the contract is silent, and reimbursement is dependent on the goodwill of the employer.

In line with the provision of uniforms to police and firefighters by employers, the issue of furnishing equipment has also arisen. Most employers provide the basic equipment needed by the employees to perform their jobs effectively, and this equipment must be returned to the employer when the employee separates from the service. But some items may not always be considered basic equipment, and here negotiations determine the outcome. Recently, the union in a police bargaining unit requested that all members of the union be furnished bulletproof vests by the employer. Because of the nature of their jobs, some police and firefighter agreements contain provisions pertaining to injury on duty, and they cover a variety of situations. Some agreements require the employer to pay in full all hospitalization and related medical expenses; others cover hypertension and heart disease, on the grounds that these illnesses are directly related to the hazards and stress of public safety occupations; some call for a special disability pension; and others provide an allowance until the employee becomes eligible for regular retirement.[14]

Sick leave is a common benefit found in both the private and the public sectors. The opportunity for "buying back" unused sick leave is becoming much more common in the public sector. The goal is to obtain part of the unused sick leave upon retirement, thereby motivating employees not to use up all their leave. Initially, many communities opposed such requests, but a growing number of bargaining units have negotiated such provisions. In the 1970s, the benefit was fairly widespread and commonly provided that upon retirement, an employee would receive a specified percentage of accumulated unused sick leave, up to a specified dollar maximum. There is substantial variation among bargaining units, but a reasonably common provision is 25 percent of accumulated unused sick leave, up to a maximum of $1,000. Some police or fire agreements provide for 50 percent of accumulated unused sick leave, with a maximum of $6,000. In some cases the maximum is set in terms of number of days, such as forty-eight days.

Redemption of unused sick leave on an annual basis has also become a relatively common monetary fringe item in the public sector. One agreement, for example, provides that an employee who has used fewer than five sick leave days in a specified twelve-month period may elect to redeem these days in a lumpsum cash payment in accordance with the following schedule:[15]

Annual Sick Days	Sick Days Used	Redemption
15	0	5
14	1	4
13	2	3
12	3	2
11	4	1
10	5	0

The employer is to notify each qualifying employee with redemption options; an employee may elect to redeem all or part of the entitlement while unredeemed sick days continue to accumulate.

Because of the nature of the work performed by police and firefighters, there are demands by the community at large, as well as by private employers, for their services beyond their normal tours of duty. Both police and firefighters have various work opportunities outside their regular assignments, and from the perspective of both the employer and the employee, guidelines and rules are important. Numerous collective bargaining agreements have provisions that refer to outside employment opportunities for the bargaining unit members. From the government's point of view, such provisions ensure the community's safety and the efficiency of the protective service, and the possibility of conflict of interest is diminished by the employer's retaining some control over outside government work. The employees benefit from such provisions in that wage levels and maximum number of hours of outside work are clearly established, as well as the means of distributing the available jobs equitably.

The vast majority of such outside employment opportunities are paid private details; employees are assigned to police- and fire-related work for private employers. These assignments may include fire watches, crowd control at sporting, entertainment, or political events, and night watch jobs at construction sites. In some situations, the need of private employers for the authority and the specialized skills of police and fire personnel derives from ordinances and laws requiring adherence to certain security standards. In other situations, private employers utilize police and fire personnel because of their own concern about safety or security of their property or enterprise or the concern of insurance companies. Regardless of the reason, private employers present personnel requests to the police or fire department, and these departments then act as referral agents. The government employer takes into account the possible impact these paid detail assignments may have on its own operations as it makes the requested assignments.

Provisions concerning outside employment in collective bargaining agreements stipulate the conditions under which an employee can be assigned to a paid private detail. The department can take into account its own staffing needs, and the types of outside jobs are generally specified. These provisions normally authorize the department to make assignments, assume equitable distribution of work opportunities for all personnel, and arrange for supervision of outside employment under specified conditions. These provisions also specify the hourly rates and the minimum number of hours for each assignment. The outside detail rate is generally either time and one-half the employee's regular hourly rate or some specific hourly rate that is approximately equivalent to time and one-half. In some cases, a dollar amount above the overtime rate is specified. Most clauses provide a minimum of four hours for any assignment, and others may require a larger guarantee. Higher premium pay is often provided for certain holiday work, hazardous duty, and police service during strikes and labor disputes.[16]

Unlike any financial benefits that private sector units bargain for, paid private detail provisions negotiated by public sector unions are cost free to the public employer. The costs are borne by the private employer, who sometimes is required by law to utilize fire or police personnel at prices fixed by someone else. Thus, outside paid details provide benefit opportunities to police and firefighter personnel at no real cost to their employer, and some employers see this as an opportunity to trade off this cost-free benefit for some other benefit that may have a direct cost on budget. (In the third case, this issue becomes critical in the negotiations of a contract up for renewal).

In addition to the paid private details, some contracts have clauses concerning paid details for work required by the public employer—for instance, police guards at road construction, special police work at a public event sponsored by the community, or a fire-watch duty assignment at a public building. These assignments are outside the normal line of duty or functions of the personnel involved. Although some public employers may reassign police or fire personnel to cover such work and pay regular time, overtime, or compensatory time, others provide for a paid detail rate that may or may not be identical with the private detail rate. In addition, some contracts contain provisions specifically permitting protective service personnel to take a second job that is not police or fire related. Such provisions do not cover wage rates or wage guarantees but deal with the rules employees must follow in seeking approval for the second job. Some contracts prohibit police officers or firefighters from engaging in part-time employment that interferes with their efficiency or availability for duty or with the health, safety, or welfare of the public.[17]

Premium pay for work on holidays is standard in the private sector and fairly common as well in most bargaining units in the public sector. Holiday pay for police units has become quite common but not for firefighters, principally because of the schedule of days and hours worked per week. Where the issue is negotiated, not

only is ...erest in the numbers of days recognized as holidays
but a... of pay received for working the holiday when it is
the ...gularly scheduled workday. For police units that
hav... work schedules from five days on and two days
o... four days on and two days off, the holiday pay
is...asing the pay from one-fifth to one-fourth of a

...ant differences between the private and the
...d to monetary fringe items. These differences
...of the special nature of some public employ-
...ature of the job functions of certain groups
...es. And where benefits for public employ-
...e difference may be substantial.

th...
area,
set in ...
were satis-
tween the
...ot live in
es, where

...ns for Discussion

... fringe benefits, what is the basis for
...r as different from the private sector?
...e benefits different, while many others
...lar in both sectors?
... the public sector handled differently
... same sector? Is this a fair system?
...; all public sector employees under civil
... attain some semblance of uniformity?
... federally mandated, civil service system
...yed by the states and local communities?
...g all public sector employees under the
...ons acts that currently cover private sec-
...why not?

l fourteen
...rs. There
...out fifty
...ment ran
... Three of
...ans; they
...ctive bar-
...he second
...signed in
...d. By this
... employ-

...he EMT Requirement

... town in
...njured in
...ealized it
...ll shifts.
...MTs, but
... special-
...y by the
... became
...eetings,
...unteered

...ll community not very close to any large
...d substantially over the past twenty years
...a "bedroom community." Most residents
... and upper middle class, and most homes
...rately large. There seems to be a great deal
... with the town's administration and ser-
...ofessional town manager was hired by the

elected town council, and the town manager was an imn
cess. He developed a good working relationship with t
he modernized the operation of the town's administrati
was well liked by the townspeople.

A short time after the arrival of the town manager,
firefighters, police, and teachers organized, and first con
signed with each bargaining unit. The town manager ha
previous labor relations experience, and the negotiation
union went well. Each of the contracts was in line with
found in comparative communities of the surrounding
the subsequent agreements followed the general patter
comparative communities. In general, the townspeople
fied with the settlements and with the good relations be
town and its unions. Many of the union members did
Newkirk but commuted from neighboring communiti
housing was more affordable.

Prior to the formation of a union, the town employe
firefighters, and this had been its size for many prior ye
was no hospital in the community, the closest being a
miles away in a neighboring city, and the town fire depar
the town ambulance when emergency service was needed
the fourteen firefighters were emergency medical technic
received no extra bonus for this, nor did the first colle
gaining agreement provide for any EMT stipend. When t
three-year agreement with the firefighters' union was
1985, an EMT stipend of $500 per year was introduce
time, the firefighters' bargaining unit had grown to twent
ees; of the six new firefighters employed, two were EMTs.

Because of three major fires with personal injuries in th
1986 and a two-car accident with five residents seriously
early 1987, the town purchased a second ambulance but
did not have sufficient EMTs to run the ambulances on
The fire chief urged more of the firefighters to become E
there was little incentive. To qualify, a person had to take
ized program on his or her own time, and the stipend pa
town for a qualified EMT was relatively small. The matter
a heated topic of discussion at a number of town council
but none of the fifteen firefighters who were not EMTs vol
to enter an EMT program.

When negotiations began for the new contract, among the town's proposals was one requiring that all firefighters become EMTs within twelve months of the date of the contract and that all must maintain EMT status; the EMT stipend would be increased from $500 to $750. The union submitted its proposals, and negotiations seemed to be going smoothly except in regard to the EMT issue. The three persons on the union negotiating team were not EMTs and did not want to become EMTs. They informally surveyed their membership and found that the eleven firefighters who were in the department before 1980 and were not EMTs all objected to having to become EMTs at this point in their careers. This was reported at a negotiating session with the town, and it was noted that these eleven who opposed the town's proposal represented a majority of the twenty members of the bargaining unit.

Tentative agreement was reached on the wage issue and on the few fringe items raised by the union, but the union appeared adamant in its opposition to the town's proposal on EMTs. The town informed the union bargaining committee that it considered its EMT proposal critical to the agreement and that no agreement could be reached until this issue was resolved. As a last resort, the town upped the EMT stipend offer to $1,000 per year, but the union continued to reject the town's proposal, and a stalemate was reached. Since all the issue were unresolved, all were submitted to fact-finding, and after a formal hearing, the fact finder issued his recommendation, which included the following on the EMT issue:

1. The EMT stipend to be increased from $500 to $1,000 on July 1, 1988, and to $1,250 on July 1, 1989.
2. Firefighters hired after the date of the signing of the agreement must be certified EMTs within eighteen months of hiring and must maintain EMT status.
3. Firefighters hired after the date of the town proposal on EMTs but before the date of signing of the agreement must become EMTs within eighteen months of hiring but may drop after five years.
4. Firefighters hired before the date of the town proposal on EMTs may do so as they like.

Discussion Issues, Problems, and Questions

1. If you were the representative of the employer in the fact-finding proceeding, what arguments would you have made to the fact finder on the employer's position on EMTs? Why had the employer upped the stipend offer for EMTs to $1,000 while still in negotiations? As an outsider, would you have considered the employer's arguments convincing?
2. If you were the representative of the union in the fact-finding proceedings, what arguments would you have made to the fact finder to defend your total opposition to the employer's proposal? As an outsider, would you have considered the union's arguments convincing?
3. Would this kind of issue be raised in the private sector? Why or why not? Who does the employer really represent at the bargaining table? How does the employer representative know what is best for his constituency?
4. Was the union representative right in rejecting the employer's proposal to raise the EMT stipend rate to $1,000 from the current rate of $500? Was the union representative really representing the union membership?
5. What do you think of the fact finder's recommendations? If you were the employer representative, would you accept them? Why or why not? If you were the union representative, would you accept them? Why or why not? How would you have improved the recommendations in order to make them more acceptable to both sides?

Case 2: The Educational Incentive Pay Issue

In Urbano, a moderate-sized city in the Midwest, the long-time mayor had been negotiating collective bargaining agreements with five bargaining units for a number of years. The police officers were the last to organize, and their first contract was a three-year agreement, effective July 1, 1977. The negotiations had been amicable. The wage increase followed the pattern that had been offered and accepted by the other four bargaining units. The agreement contained the standard fringe benefits that were found in police agreements around the state; however, since educational incentive pay was not common in the state, there was no such benefit in the Urbano agreement.

At the time of the 1977 agreement, there were eighty police officers in the department, approximately half of them in their forties and early fifties. There had been little incentive for them to pursue any education beyond high school, and only a few of the eighty officers had more than a high school diploma. By early 1980, the force had expanded to ninety officers, and of the ten newly hired officers, four had the bachelor's degree and four had the associate's degree. At the same time, there seemed to be a growing movement across the state (as well as the nation) to upgrade the educational level of police personnel. In the negotiations for the 1980–1983 agreement, the mayor proposed that all new police hired have at least an associate's degree in police science. The union opposed the proposal, and in the negotiations over other terms of the agreement, a compromise on educational incentive pay was reached. The parties agreed on a clause that provided a $300 bonus annually for anyone having or attaining an associate's degree and a $600 bonus annually for anybody having or attaining a bachelor's degree. This provision was in line with a growing number of police contracts in the state. In view of the relatively small number of police officers with education beyond high school, the immediate cost of this provision to Urbano was relatively small.

In the negotiations for the 1983 contract, substantial wage and vacation increases were agreed upon, and no reference was made by either party to the educational incentive pay. However, five of the younger officers had gone back to school and attained the associate's degree; they were now eligible for the educational bonus. From July 1983 to the time of the start of negotiations for the 1986–1989 contract, in the spring of 1986, the police department had hired ten additional officers, eight of whom had either an associate's or a bachelor's degree. Additionally, ten more of the younger officers had attained the associate's degree. Thus, thirty-six of the one-hundred officers had advanced degrees and were receiving an annual educational bonus.

In preparing its list of demands for the 1986 negotiations, the union held a membership meeting to discuss the various issues. Police officers who already had an associate's or bachelor's degree and younger officers who had started or planned to start an educational program vigorously supported a significant increase in educational attainment benefits plus employer payment for the costs of the education. Many of the older officers, who were not likely to return to school for an additional degree and were benefiting from the longevity pay in the contract were opposed to increased educational bonuses; they realized they could not gain by any educational incentive pay, which might be gotten at the cost of not gaining in their longevity pay plan. The younger officers argued that all members of the force could take advantage of an educational incentive plan, whereas the longevity plan paid off only after many years of service, and not to the younger officers at all. The older members argued that they were too old to go back to school and that years of experience was a more important criterion for additional benefits. The compromise agreed to by the two factions in the union was to demand substantial increases in both the educational incentive pay and the longevity pay.

In preparing for the negotiations, the mayor discussed the potential issues with the members of the city council. The matter of educational incentive pay came up, and again, the proposal drafted was that all new police hired have at least an associate's degree. The city was prepared to raise the bonus to $450 for an associate's degree and $1,000 for a bachelor's degree. The city decided it would oppose any increase in longevity pay.

The union negotiating committee consisted of three union officers (all old-timers, in favor of longevity pay) and two elected members who had bachelor's degrees. After five negotiating sessions with the mayor and his committee, the wage adjustment issue and most fringe benefit issues were tentatively agreed upon. What remained were some language changes, the educational incentive pay, and longevity pay. The city continued to argue for its position on educational incentive pay, with no change in longevity pay. The union argued for substantial increases in both. After two more negotiating sessions in which only these two issues were discussed, the parties reached a tentative agreement: the educational incentive plan would provide $250 after thirty course credits, $550 for an associate's degree, and $1,200 for a bachelor's degree. The longevity plan would provide $500 after fifteen years of service (up from $400) and $750 after twenty-five years of service (up from

$550). All the negotiators felt this was about the best deal that could be worked out.

The following week, the terms of the tentative agreement were presented to the union membership for ratification, and most items quickly won general approval. However, when it came to the additional pay, the older officers, who preferred higher longevity pay allowances, charged that the younger officers had received favored treatment through the educational incentive pay. By a majority of ten votes, the tentative agreement was rejected, with the advice that the city had to come through with higher longevity pay. The parties thus had to start negotiations anew.

Discussion Issues, Problems, and Questions

1. How do you explain the mayor's strong favoritism for educational incentive pay and his opposition to longevity pay? Do you think the mayor knew of the split feelings by the union membership on the educational incentive pay? If he knew about the split, why did he not split the benefits more evenly? Is this kind of incident likely to occur in the private sector? Why or why not?
2. There seems to be a basic split in the union between the older and younger officers. How would you advise the union to resolve this problem? What impact could a split have on the operation of the police force? What should the mayor and the city do about the problem?
3. In view of the rejection of the tentative agreement by the union membership, the parties went back into negotiations to work out an agreement acceptable to the union membership. If costs are a restraint on the city's offer, could the city offer more in longevity pay without taking away some of the educational incentive pay previously agreed to? What kind of a deal would you recommend to the parties when they go back into negotiations?

Case 3: Paid Private Details

Corona, a moderate-sized industrial city on the East Coast, had shown considerable economic growth and activity. In addition, the city appeared to be a sports mecca, with a number of private sports arenas and considerable sports activities at a number of private schools. As a result, there were many opportunities for paid private details for police personnel. Details were also worked for other departments in the city, and they were paid at a time and one-half rate when the work was in excess of regular hours worked on any day or in excess of regularly scheduled workweek in any payroll week.

The city employed two hundred police officers, and most earned additional income by working paid details. The city and the police union had been engaged in a collective bargaining relationship for twenty-odd years, and although contract negotiations were sometimes difficult and long, the relations were generally good. The police chief had come up from the ranks and was held to be a good and fair administrator. Six years ago, just prior to the substantial growth in the city, the parties had negotiated a new contract that included a significant raise in the paid detail rate. The new clause provided for a time and one-half rate, instead of a flat dollar rate, in the public sector, with the minimum number of hours increased from three to four. The private detail rate was increased to time and one-half plus five dollars per hour, with a four-hour minimum. With these changes and the substantial growth of private detail opportunities, many of the police officers, especially the younger ones, began working more and more paid details, and the outside earnings of some approached their regular salaries. Inasmuch as these details meant that some officers were putting in very long hours, there was concern about the efficiency of these officers and their regular police tours of duty.

The police chief held informal discussions with the officers who were taking large numbers of paid detail assignments, indicating his concern to them and to union officials. Although there were no contractual provisions or police department rules that limited the number of details on which officers could work, the police chief indicated he might have to place a limit, for the efficiency of the department.

Negotiations began in February 1990 for a new contract; the existing contract was to expire on June 30, 1990. At the first session, the union submitted its list of demands. Included was a demand for improvements in the private detail rate. Having been made aware of the city's concern about the amount of paid detail the officers were working and feeling that the city might propose a limit on the number of detail hours an officer could work, the union proposed the following:

1. The paid detail rate shall be one and one-half times the maximum police officer rate of pay plus ten dollars per hour.
2. The rate shall be two dollars per hour higher on Sundays and legal holidays.
3. The minimum guarantee for a paid detail shall be four hours work or four hours pay.
4. In private details where liquor is served, the minimum guarantee shall be six hours of work or six hours of pay.
5. In private details, overtime rates at time and one-half the detail rate shall be charged for hours worked over eight and hours worked between midnight and 7:00 A.M.
6. In private details, where requested by an employer to protect person or property in a labor dispute, the detail rate shall be double the usual rate.

The city proposed that the police chief have the authority to limit the number of paid detail hours an officer could work in any week, in order to ensure the efficiency of the police force.

This issue of paid detail came up for discussion at the seventh bargaining session, after many of the wage and monetary fringe benefits had been tentatively settled. There had been some difficult bargaining over the wage adjustment and over the educational incentive pay, and the parties were somewhat on edge. The city argued that it had to control excessive paid details for the efficiency of the police department; no person could work over eighty hours a week, week in and week out, and still perform regular duties in a highly efficient manner. The union said that it had confidence in the current police chief's making of fair and equitable decisions on the amount and distribution of paid detail opportunities, but he was retiring in about one year. The union voiced concern about any new police chief who would be authorized to limit the amount of paid detail work an officer could accept. In defense of its proposals on paid details, the union argued that the additional costs for city departments were minimal and that there were no additional costs to the city in private detail rates. The city argued that the police chief already had authority to limit paid details for the efficiency of the department and its proposal made this authority specific. Further, the city argued, many of the private details were required by city ordinance, and therefore the city had some responsibility for higher costs to the private enterprises. Even where private details were not required by law but were requested voluntarily, the city maintained it had some responsibility for the higher costs.

Because the issue of increased longevity pay allowance also remained unsettled, the parties called in a state mediator. After three more sessions with the mediator, the parties reached a tentative agreement, which was then taken back to the required constituency for ratification. The private detail rate was improved somewhat, and the police chief retained authority to limit the number of details in any one week. There was no change in longevity pay. The mayor presented the tentative agreement to the city council, and after an explanation of various issues, the tentative agreement was unanimously ratified. The union negotiating committee presented the tentative agreement to the union membership and recommended its ratification. There was considerable opposition by a number of older police officers who took only a limited number of paid details and who favored higher longevity stipends for long-term employees. After a long debate, the tentative agreement was ratified by a 60 percent vote in favor.

Discussion Issues, Problems, and Questions

1. In the public sector, the practice of outside paid details is basically limited to police and firefighters—both of whom have a responsibility for the public safety. Is there a counterpart in the private sector? Consider specialized repair workers of electrical power or gas utility companies who are sent out to answer the emergency call of an employer or a home owner who smells gas inside a building? Why do such workers in the private sector not receive the equivalent of a policemen's detail pay?
2. If there is something special about outside detail work for police and firefighters, who should set the wage rates for such work? Should the private employers participate in the wage setting? How would the participation be arranged, and if so, how can it be done in advance of the need for the work? Should all private

employers be required to pay the identical detail rate? If the negotiations over the detail rates are between the city and the unions, what incentives are there for the city to keep the rate low? If you were the negotiator for the city, would you be tempted to negotiate a deal where the detail rate goes up while the education and longevity rates that the city pays remain stable?

3. If you were called in as a fact finder in the Corona police union negotiations to make recommendations on the last two issues— paid details and longevity pay—what would you recommend? Do you believe your recommendations are fair to both the younger police officers, who are anxious to earn as much as possible through detail work, and the older officers, who have a strong preference for earning more money through an improved longevity plan? Are your recommendations also fair to the outside private employers who have to pay detail rates? Would you recommend that the police chief be given explicit authority to limit the amount of outside detail work an officer may do in a week? If so, should there be any exceptions during emergencies? Should there be a fixed rule applying to all officers, regardless of age?

Nonmonetary Contractual Provisions

A wage proposal or fringe benefit is frequently the item that gains the greatest publicity in a collective bargaining situation, but other provisions may be critical to the signing of an agreement. To an employer, a strong management's rights clause may be worth a considerable amount of money in a trade-off with a wage increase. To a union, a security provision may be worth more than some wage increase. To both parties, the scope of bargaining is a crucial nonmonetary provisions in any contract. The employer will argue for a narrow scope, leaving more items in management's sole discretion, while the union will argue for as wide a scope as possible, placing more topics in the collective bargaining arena. There may be little immediate cost to a scope of bargaining provision, but the long-run impact of the kinds of issues that can be negotiated may be great.

The most limited scope of bargaining is found in the federal government; state laws require bargaining over wages, hours, and important conditions of employment. The issues of scope generally involve management rights. In education, for example, controversial issues include class size, decisions to grant or deny tenure, assignments, schedules, and transfers from one school or subject to another—all matters that managements frequently contend are vital to doing their job well.[1] In some states, matters that are considered inherent items of management prerogatives are illegal topics of bargaining. The position of teachers' unions on this matter was best presented by the president of the American Federation of Teachers in 1965:

> We would place no limit on the scope of negotiations—the items which are subject to the bargaining process. Anything on which the two parties can agree should become a part of the agreement. . . .
>
> I look for a great expansion in the effective scope of negotiations. . . . Obviously, class sizes, number of classes taught, curriculum, hiring standards, textbooks and supplies, extracurricular activities—in fact anything having to do with the operation of the school is a matter for professional concern and thus should be subject to collective bargaining.[2]

Because of the role of education in the United States, state laws vary significantly with respect to the scope of bargaining for public school teachers. In some states, legislation requires each teacher to have a duty-free lunch period; where such laws do not exist, teachers are often required to supervise students during their lunch hour. States require schools to be open a certain number of hours each day, and some laws regulate the maximum size of classes in both secondary and elementary schools. Minimum length of school terms is provided in the state constitutions of a number of states.[3]

For other state employees, the scope of bargaining is relatively broad in most states. There are limitations in most states and for most bargaining units, but the limits are not as stringent as those for federal employees. Nevertheless, some states have placed special limits on bargaining for public employer groups such as police and firefighters. In one state, for example, legislation provides that "no municipal employer shall be required to negotiate over subjects of minimum manning of shift coverage, with any employee organization representing municipal police officers and firefighters."[4]

Many of the nonmonetary provisions of public sector collective bargaining agreements are similar to the provisions in private sector agreements. Provisions pertaining to matters such as union security and dues checkoff vary little between public and private collective bargaining agreements. In general, there is little difference between the public and private sector agreements in matters such as equal distribution of overtime and the right of employees to refuse overtime. However, public employees such as teachers, police, and firefighters have many relatively unique working conditions and situations that evolve into nonmonetary provisions in their collective bargaining contracts.

Supervisors in the Bargaining Unit

Because of the professionalism of public school teachers and the history of teachers' associations, first-line supervisors, whether principals or department heads, often do not act as supervisors. The issue that arises is whether such supervisors should be in the bargaining unit of classroom teachers and be permitted to be members in the organization that acts as bargaining agent for the classroom teachers, or whether they should be separate units. Working conditions of teachers are often affected by state laws that require schools to be open a certain number of hours each day and a specified number of days in the school year. In a growing number of agreements, however, teachers' unions have negotiated the matters of class size, team teaching, and transfer privileges for tenured teachers, items clearly not relevant in the private sector. In some instances, teachers' unions have also negotiated the length of the school day and the number of teaching periods in a day.

Work Schedule

For some groups of employees, the work schedule may be an important nonmonetary condition. Because of the nature of the work and the requirement of constant coverage, police officers and firefighters have work schedules that vary significantly from those of the average public sector employee and the average private sector employee. In the mid-1970s a substantial portion of collective bargaining agreements covering police officers and firefighters contained no clauses stipulating scheduled weekly hours; in contracts that specified the weekly hours, over half designated hours over forty, with the largest number at fifty-six hours. These longer workweek schedules usually provided that employees be divided into platoons, each assigned to twenty-four-hour daily schedules that alternated day on and day off or established rotating tours of ten and fourteen hours. In addition, it was common practice in the private sector agreement to specify the number of days in a workweek, but it was an exception in police and fire contracts. At this time, some firefighters' contracts called for platoons to work twenty-four hours on duty and forty-eight hours off duty; others provided that the normal work schedule was to be four days on and two days off and then five days on and two days off, on a rotating schedule.[5]

More recently, a substantial number of collective bargaining contracts with public safety employees have lowered the workweek to approximately forty hours. The hours of work provision of a recent police agreement provides the following:[6]

> *Section 1. Work Week Schedule*: Employees shall be scheduled by the Police Chief to work on regular work shifts; regularly scheduled work shifts shall not exceed forty (40) in one (1) week except as hereinafter provided for in Section 2. . . .
>
> *Section 2*: Regularly scheduled work shifts . . . will be based on four (4) consecutive days of work and two (2) consecutive days off. For employees thus affected, the regularly scheduled work shifts shall not exceed thirty-two (32) hours in any six (6) day period.

With slight variations, many police units have a schedule of four consecutive days of work and two consecutive days off.[7]

The more common provision of scheduled hours of work for firefighters is an average of forty-two hours per week. One agreement provides the following:

(a) The regular weekly schedule for all employees shall consist of an average of forty-two (42) hours a week. . . .
(b) The hours of duty for the Fire Fighting force . . . shall be worked by four groups working a ten (10) hour day tour and a fourteen (14) hour night on the rotating schedule which became effective . . . 1970.[8]

The schedule sample included in the agreement indicates that an employee works two ten-hour-day tours, has one day off, then two fourteen-hour night tours, then three days off, at which point the cycle is repeated. One aspect of this issue is addressed in Case 2 of this chapter.

These different types of work schedules for police and firefighters clearly indicate the uniqueness of the duties and job requirements of security personnel. In almost all contracts, explicitly or implicitly, these schedules can be changed by the police chief or the fire chief in emergencies. Additionally, police chiefs and fire chiefs are given considerable leeway in making significant changes in contract terms in emergencies. Most often it is a judgment call by the chief, and police officers and firefighters are required to accept the change, although they may protest later.

Managing the Work Force

It is generally assumed that the wages of police and firefighters take into account the danger involved in the work. Nevertheless, there are nonmonetary provisions that can provide some additional sense of security. One such item involves managing. Years ago, it was relatively rare for a collective bargaining contract to stipulate the number of employees necessary to operate a police or fire station or a piece of equipment such as a patrol car or a fire truck. Recently, this matter has become more common in contracts, as police and firefighters pressure for their inclusion in the bargaining process. Most such provisions relate to the staffing of a specific unit or piece of equipment; rarely do they relate to minimum staffing of shift coverage, which many states consider a management responsibility. In many jurisdictions, it is a permissible subject of negotiation but not a required one.

The position of police and firefighter's unions on the issue of staffing, on both equipment and shift, has been advocated on the grounds of personal safety. Having an extra officer as backup in a serious emergency is a matter that many unions battle frequently, arguing it is safety insurance. Minimum staffing can also have financial gains to members, in the form of more overtime and more work for more officers. From the perspective of the employer, such provisions are a cost; they must either hire additional personnel or use existing personnel on overtime at premium rates.

Teachers' unions have pushed similarly hard for the inclusion in the scope of bargaining of such items as class size, preparation time, and teaching loads. Teachers have argued for these provisions not in terms of their own convenience or comfort; rather, they hold that such provisions will result in more appropriate work loads for teachers and an improved education for the students. Employers who oppose the inclusion of such provisions in the collective bar-

travel outside the town of Westborough in relation to the physical condition.[11]

This collective bargaining agreement also established an advisory committee of three members of the union to meet with the police chief at least once every three months "to discuss and make recommendations for improvements of the general health and safety of the employees."

Physical Fitness

As more parties to collective bargaining agreements agreed to authorize management to require, under a specified set of circumstances, employees to undergo physical examinations, there developed interest in the positive aspect of this problem: physical fitness. A growing number of contracts provide for physical fitness programs, and in some cases, all employees are required to participate in the program. One such agreement on a physical fitness program reads as follows:

> The Town and the Union agree that there should be physical fitness standards and an on-duty physical fitness program for members of the bargaining unit. The formulation of the specific standards and programs shall be determined by the Labor/Management Committee established herein. It is understood by the parties that the physical fitness standards are not intended by the Town to be a cause for layoff or retirement, or affect promotions of the members of the bargaining unit.
>
> After the formulation of the physical fitness standards as determined above, the Committee will then set the procedures for determining if the standards are being met and establish a suitable on duty physical fitness program designed to develop or maintain fitness.[12]

This labor agreement went on to provide for physical fitness equipment:

> The Employer will provide a one time sum of money equal to two thousand dollars ($2,000.00) multiplied by the number of fire stations in the town of Brookline. Such money will be used for the purchase of physical fitness equipment to be installed in each fire station and to be available for voluntary use by employees in each

station. The nature of such equipment will be determined by the Union and the Employer.

The principle of physical fitness is not something that police or firefighters' unions oppose. Both parties agree that public safety officers should be physically fit to perform their job. The matters of concern to unions are the standards of physical fitness and who is to establish the standards. They are concerned that physical fitness standards may affect promotions of injured employees or older employees unless safeguards are included to prevent such negative effects. Thus, when an employer proposes a physical fitness program, the negotiations are generally over the safeguards the union wants to protect the program from being used to affect certain groups of employees negatively.

Nonsmoking Provisions

Another health factor that appears to have grown in importance in recent years is smoking. If the cost of health insurance is rising rapidly, is not smoking one of the factors causing health problems? As more and more public sector employers show concern about physical examinations and physical fitness programs, there has been a recent realization that smoking is injurious to health. In a number of jurisdictions, public service employers have unilaterally issued regulations prohibiting police officers and firefighters from smoking on the job. Unions charge that the no-smoking rules have changed the working rules unilaterally, thereby violating their labor agreement. Where police employers have brought the issue to the bargaining table, unions have argued that a no-smoking rule would violate the rights of individual employees and change the conditions of employment of officers who had been smoking prior to their appointment as a police officer or a firefighter.

No-smoking provisions are not common in collective bargaining agreements of police or firefighters. One such provision reads as follows:

> Police officers shall not smoke at any time when on-duty. This requirement shall not constitute a condition of employment for all police officers. Any police officer violating this action shall be sub-

ject to disciplinary action by the Town. The provisions of this article shall not apply to any full-time police officer appointed to July 1, 1982.[13]

The parties apparently were willing to exclude from the non-smoking rule police officers who had been appointed prior to July 1, 1982. What issues or matters were traded off by the union and by the employer to obtain this compromise resolution are unknown; however, when these parties negotiated their next agreement, the no-smoking provision was expanded to employees hired prior to July 1, 1982.[14]

If the smoking issue is to have a significant effect on the health and health care of public safety employees, it cannot be limited to a prohibition from smoking while on duty. This is the approach that some public employers have taken, and proposals have been made in the negotiation process to limit employment in the police force and in the fire department to nonsmokers. Unions have strongly opposed such proposals on a number of grounds. They note that smoking tobacco is not a violation of the law, and therefore putting the activity of tobacco smoking in the same category as drugs is patently unfair. On a civil liberties ground, the unions contend that refusing to employ an otherwise qualified applicant as a police officer or a firefighter because he or she smokes at home violates the person's civil liberties and deprives the applicant of a job in a discriminatory fashion. Depriving current employees of the right to smoke off the job, the unions contend, not only violates civil liberties but also involves a change in conditions of employment without the consent of the union. Unions argue further that a no-smoking rule limited to new employees would involve discrimination and would create an impossible situation between new employees and old-time employees.

This issue has not been resolved in sufficient jurisdictions to predict its long-run results. However, it seems likely that public employers will continue to propose and promote no-smoking rules for all public safety employees, and unions will continue to oppose the broad rule that prohibits smoking for all employees at all times. If health benefit costs continue to soar, there is little doubt that some compromise resolution will evolve. One possibility is the establishment of differentiated insurance rates between groups that prohibit smoking and those that do not. Another possibility is to establish lower rates for nonsmokers.

Health Problems and Benefits

Some police and firefighters' unions have taken the offensive on the matter of the health of their members. The inherent health hazards of the duties performed by firefighters have been publicized, and in some jurisdictions they have gained sufficient public support to do something about the hazards of their job duties. In Massachusetts, for example, the state legislature passed an act in 1990 "creating a rebuttable presumption of job relatedness for firefighters in the Commonwealth suffering from certain disabling conditions of cancer."[15] This piece of legislation, referred to as the cancer presumption act, provides in part:

(1) . . . Any condition of cancer affecting the skin or the central nervous, lymphatic, digestive, hematological, urinary, skeletal, oral or prostrate systems, resulting in a total disability or death to a uniformed member of a paid fire department . . . , shall, if he successfully passed a physical examination on entry into such services or subsequent to each entry, which examination failed to reveal any evidence of such conditions, be presumed to have been suffered in line of duty, unless it is shown by a preponderance of the evidence that non-service connected risk factors or non-service connected accidents or hazards undergone, or any combination thereof, caused such incapacity. . . .

(2) The provisions of this section shall not apply to any person serving such positions for fewer than five years at the time that such condition is first discovered, or should have been discovered. . . .

(3) The provisions of this section shall also apply to any condition of cancer . . . which, in general, may result from exposure to heat or radiation or to a known or suspected carcinogen.

This law unquestionably gives firefighters certain health benefits that are not easily attainable through the collective bargaining process. However, it may strengthen the municipal employer's hand in negotiating a no-smoking provision with a firefighters' union. The presumption of job-related cancer may be rebuttable if the employee has been a heavy smoker for many years.

Drug Testing

Public employers have attempted to introduce drug testing programs in an effort to reduce health insurance costs and respond to public concern about the possible use by public safety personnel of drugs and alcohol. There has been considerable discussion about the testing of various occupational groups for drugs and alcohol and the conditions under which these tests should be made. The focus of the national media has been on airline pilots, air traffic controllers, and railroad and transit motor workers, occupations in which an accident may involve large numbers of persons.

There appear to be relatively few police and firefighter labor contracts that contain drug testing provisions, but the numbers have been increasing. One estimate is that about 13 percent of police contracts and about 15 percent of firefighters' contracts contain some type of drug testing provision.[16]

The use of drug testing by public employers of police and firefighters is undoubtedly more widespread than the practice represented by provisions in collective bargaining agreements. There undoubtedly is widespread use of preemployment drug screening, which would not necessarily be mentioned in the labor agreement. In addition, public employers may attempt unilaterally to institute a formal or informal drug testing program even if the labor agreement is silent on the issue. Such programs might be justified as falling within the ambit of broadly phrased management rights clauses or clauses requiring employees to submit to periodic physical examinations.

There is no standard drug testing program in the provisions of labor contracts. Most specify the type of test to be used, and the most common one is urinalysis, although blood tests and breathalyzers are also used. All provisions provide that testing is allowed for probable cause, although there is variation in the language as to what is probable cause. Many provisions also allow testing under other conditions, including random testing, postaccident testing, and prepromotion testing. Most provisions also make available some type of rehabilitation. One such labor agreement provision, entitled, "Substance Abuse Program," stipulates:

> The purpose of this program is to establish the fact that the City of North Adams and its employees have the right to expect a drug free environment in the work place. The main emphasis of the program is not to be punishment, but of counseling and rehabilitation of employees with a problem of alcoholism or drug-dependency.
>
> No initial drug testing shall be permitted in a random or universal matter, except as hereafter provided. Testing shall only be permitted where there is both reason to suspect drug or alcohol use and evidence that this suspected use is affecting job performance. An employee has the right to union representation with regard to all drug and alcohol testing issues. Drug and alcohol testing shall be permitted based upon a reasonable suspicion standard.[17]

In another collective bargaining agreement, a provision entitled "Drug Screening" reads, in part:

(1) The Chief of Police, upon probable cause based upon an officer's conduct, may require a police officer to submit a test sample for drug screening by means of blood analysis to detect the presence of non-prescribed drugs or controlled substances. A test sample must thereafter be provided upon the Chief's request.
(2) The affected officer may initiate a review of the Chief's directive. If requested, the Chief's directive shall be reviewed by a special panel. . . . The purpose of the review is to decide only whether the Chief has information which establishes probable cause to request screening.[18]

In one provision pertaining to "intoxicants," no specific test is mentioned, and if a proceeding occurs against an employee, the union agrees not to take part. This provision reads in part:

> The Union and the City hereby agree that no employee of the City's Fire Department, while on duty should be under the influence of an intoxicant and to be under such influence would only tarnish the good reputation of the Fire Department and that of its employ-

ees. Both parties hereby further agree that the lives and property of citizens are put on an added risk and fellow employees performance is also impaired. . . .

The penalty for an employee found guilty of being under the influence of an intoxicant shall be at the discretion of the Appointing Authority. Any penalty invoked can be the subject for appeal by the employee involved. . . . The Union hereby affirms that it will neither interfere on the part in any process that may arrive [*sic*] as a result of any provisions contained in this Article.[19]

In another community, the town and the firefighters jointly agreed to a drug testing policy and incorporated it into their collective bargaining agreement. This policy provides for limited random drug testing:

The Fire Chief may, to the extent he considers necessary for the safe and productive conduct of municipal business and public safety, perform random drug screening inspections of employees as mentioned herein to determine whether an employee is under the influence of drugs or controlled substances while under the control or subject to the requirements of the Fire Department . . . its Fire Chief, or his designee. . . .

The selection procedure for such random screening will be governed by a secured computer selection process. The selection of individual personnel to be screened will be effected by a computer program designed for a random selection of personnel on the basis of a one year cycle.[20]

Although drug testing for probable cause is becoming rather common in labor agreements covering police officers and firefighters, random testing is still rather unusual. However, the issue of random testing is arising more frequently, with strong public support, and police and firefighters unions will have to decide how they will negotiate with employers over this issue.

Rehabilitation Programs

Because alcoholism and drug abuse often affect the work force and the workplace, there has been a recent trend of employers' establishing rehabilitation programs, with the cooperation of unions. Many large employers in the private sector and some government employers have established such employee assistance programs in an effort to help rehabilitate employees with such problems as alcoholism, drug abuse, mental health, and financial stress. These programs vary considerably, but most often the employer provides an office where specialized professional personnel are available to discuss and provide assistance to an employee on a confidential basis. An employee may be referred to the program by a supervisor or may enter the program with no referral. It is generally understood that participation in such a program will not reflect negatively on the employee's personnel record or employment status. In all such instances, the aim is rehabilitation of the employee, at no cost to the employee.

A recent study indicates that in 1990, over 12 percent of collective bargaining agreements in the public sector provided for special programs of employee assistance.[21]

Residency Requirements

An issue that has a history going back to the depression of the 1930s is one requiring public service employees to reside in the community in which they work. This policy was adopted by communities that felt that it did not seem appropriate to hire someone from outside the area when many local citizens were out of work. This practice was fairly common until the 1950s and 1960s, when public service employment expanded, but salaries did not keep pace with those of the private sector. Many communities had to ignore or abandon such regulations in order to recruit and hold qualified personnel.[22]

Most residency rules were established before collective bargaining came common for public sector employees. The matter became an issue in collective bargaining when public employee organizations attempted to negotiate the removal or the modification of residency rules. Over time, most residency rules disappeared, except in the case of public safety employees, where some rationale for their continuance seemed to exist. In reference to police, the argument was advanced that the personal involvement of police officers in the life of the city might contribute to their dedication and improve their performance. In reference to firefighters, the argument was advanced that residing in the city would make them more available in an emergency.

Modifications of the strict residency rules sometimes limited hiring to local citizens, although once employed, they were free to relocate. Other variations required employees to live within a convenient distance from their work stations so that they would be available in an emergency. In some cases, distance was measured as distance from the employee's work station, and in other cases, the limit of residence was defined in terms of commuting time. In other situations, residency was limited to the city where employed or to any city or town contiguous to the city where employed. In one Massachusetts community about a mile from the New Hampshire border, the town and its police union negotiated a residency provision that required that anyone hired reside within Massachusetts and within a fifteen-mile radius of the town.

Most residency rules currently found in collective bargaining agreements pertain to firefighters. Some public employers feel very strongly about having firefighters live in the community, so as to be readily available in case of a callback in an emergency. For a variety of reasons, firefighters' unions frequently oppose residency requirements. In many well-to-do communities, housing is beyond the reach of many public service employees. In some situations, the local public school system is perceived as inadequate, and firefighters prefer living elsewhere. Sometimes the social atmosphere is such that some firefighters prefer to commute rather than live in the community. The residency provisions in labor agreements vary significantly depending on the priority given to this principle by the employer and the relative strength of the opposition of the union. A residency requirement is not a major nonmonetary provision in a labor agreement, but it can become large and important for public sector employees under various sets of conditions.

Roll Call

A relatively unique working condition that affects police officers is roll call. Because of the nature of police service and the need for police coverage, there has been a longstanding practice of an overlap of shifts. This means, for example, that there is an overlap of time of first- and second-shift employees, of second- and third-shift employees, and of third- and first-shift employees. The collective bargaining process did not stop the practice, but in many police collective bargaining negotiations, the issue involves the amount of time of the overlap for roll call and when the roll call should begin. The most common type of overlap is fifteen minutes, but ten minutes is not uncommon. Regardless of the amount of time of the overlap, employees are paid for this time, generally at the rate of time and one-half their regular wage. Where the overlap is fifteen minutes and the employees are paid at time and one-half, this amounts to an additional 4.7 percent of their regular wage, guaranteed every day worked. In a number of instances, the issue also involves when the roll call should begin—before the start of the shift or after the end of it. For example, if the hours of the first shift are from 7:00 A.M. to 3:00 A.M., should the employees of this shift be required to come in at 6:45 A.M. for fifteen minutes of roll call (and overlap with the previous shift employees) or be required to stay until 3:15 P.M. for fifteen minutes of roll call (and overlap with the next shift)? The police chief may have a preference; so may employees, and the matter may have to be negotiated. In Case 4 the issue of roll-call time is critical to the negotiations.

Miscellaneous Provisions

Some of the nonmonetary provisions in collective bargaining agreements in the public sector exist because of the structure and administrative authority of the public sector employer and others because of the relatively unique duties and functions of the employees involved. Although many of these provisions do not involve direct monetary benefits to the employees or direct monetary costs to the employer, many of them provide psychological or indirect benefits to one party or to both. (In the private sector, many provisions are also affected by the technical and market environment of the particular sector.)

Another issue that does not quite fit into the rubric of monetary benefits is one that limits the number of hours worked by police officers. These limits may curtail the earning opportunities of police officers and also pose substantial costs to the employer if additional police must be employed. This issue may arise because both the community and police unions agree that the safety of the officers and the public is of paramount importance and that police work is stressful. Using such a rationale, parties sometimes negotiate a cap on the hours an officer may work in a twenty-four-hour period and in a week. The common limitation is that no employee may work more than twelve hours in a twenty-four-hour period or more than fifty-six hours in one weekly pay period. Typically included in this cap are all overtime hours and hours worked on paid detail; exceptions are permitted in cases of emergency as declared by the chief of police. Where a contractual gap does not exist, the police chief normally has the authority to limit the hours worked by virtue of his or her right to assign overtime work and to authorize paid detail work.

Where police officers perceive work (and therefore earning) opportunities beyond the contractual gap and the chief fails to grant exception, police unions may attempt to raise the cap on the daily or weekly limitations, or on both. Adjustment in the daily cap from twelve to sixteen hours is not too uncommon; less common is raising the weekly cap to sixty-four hours.

Questions for Discussion

1. What are some of the major nonmonetary provisions in labor contracts that are considered important by both public and private sector unions? by both public and private employers? Why are some of these issues of equal importance in both sectors?

2. Are the nonmonetary provisions of the collective bargaining agreement any less important than many of the monetary benefits? Why are some nonmonetary matters of crucial importance to either the union or the public employer? (Note that what appears to be a nonmonetary item to a union may involve significant costs to an employer.)

3. Why is outside detail work important to some employers and not to others? If you were a town administrator negotiating over an outside detail rate, how would you handle the issue? Would you be willing to settle for a substantially higher detail rate in order to achieve a smaller settlement in wages for the police officers?

4. Many nonmonetary provisions are occupation specific; that is,

they apply to police officers but not to firefighters, or vice versa. If a dollar value cannot be placed on the provision, how can the police union and the firefighter union be treated equally? What if the past practice has been to grant both unions equal wage and fringe adjustments?

5. Because of the nature of the work, the police chief and the fire chief normally have considerable authority over the conditions of employment when they declare an emergency. If you were a police chief, how would you view the proposal to raise the limitations of hours worked from fifty-six to sixty-four per week? How would you respond to the argument that some police officers hold part-time jobs in the private sector and these hours worked are not counted under the gap?

Case 1: Wage Increases and Layoffs

The town of Delta has had a collective bargaining relationship with its teachers, police officers, firefighters, and general municipal employees for thirty-five years. The town administrator, appointed fifteen years ago, developed a good working relationship with the leaders of the various public sector unions that negotiated with the town. Economic conditions in the nation and the region had been good, and the town was in an excellent financial situation. Over the years, the unions had negotiated substantial wage and fringe benefit adjustments, in excess of the gains made by the private sector unions in the general area.

In 1988, after about fifteen years of substantial gains, the situation changed; the area fell into a serious recession, and the town was extremely hard-pressed financially. In negotiating its contract in early 1990, the firefighters' union, which normally led in settlements with the town, was offered a zero wage increase over the two years of the contract and no layoffs, or, as an alternative, a wage increase of 2 percent in each of the two years but an immediate layoff of 10 percent of the work force. After long, hard bargaining between the union and the town, and among various groups within the union, the parties agreed on a zero wage increase and no layoffs. The police union immediately signed an identical agreement.

Historically, the other town unions not only followed the firefighters' settlement in time but also in the pattern of wage adjustments. In 1990 the teachers' union had already begun contract negotiations with the town when the firefighters reached their agreement. The teachers' union now faced a dilemma: should it continue to follow the lead of the firefighters, which would mean no wage increase for two years, or break the pattern and take a wage increase, with layoffs?

The teachers held a number of meetings, both formal and informal, to discuss the options that their union faced. Some of the members had secure jobs and advocated taking the wage increase; they needed the extra income and believed that such a settlement would put their union in a leadership role. However, younger teachers were clearly concerned; if the union settled for a wage increase, it would be at the expense of their jobs. Although the school superintendent did not disclose what he would do with a smaller number of teachers, it seemed likely that he would have to increase the number of students per class. Clearly there was no unanimity among the teachers over this matter. Some viewed maintaining small classes as a principal factor in providing quality education. Others were not convinced that larger classes would jeopardize the quality of education, and they were prepared to accept larger classes in exchange for a wage increase.

Discussion Issues, Problems, and Questions

1. If you were a senior teacher with tenure in the school system, what would you advise the union negotiating committee to do on this matter? Would the extra wage mean more to you than a job for one of your fellow teachers? How would your family react to a wage settlement of no increase for two years?
2. If you were a junior teacher in the school system who might be laid off if the union negotiated a wage increase, what would your reaction be to your fellow teachers while you were still in the school system? If there were free and open discussion of the issue at union meetings and you knew which teachers were in favor of taking a wage increase (at the expense of junior members' jobs), how would you react to them in terms of normal contact during the school day?
3. Was the town wrong in offering the union alternatives that

inevitably pit one group of teachers against another? Should the town have made a determination of what was best for the community and its school system and then offered only that alternative? Would this have decreased the resultant open feuding within the union?

4. If you were concerned only with providing the best education possible for the town's children, what would you have advised the town administrator before he began negotiations with the teachers?

Case 2: Work Schedules and More Time Off

For many years the firefighters' union and the city of Alpha have had a collective bargaining relationship, with both parties reasonably satisfied with the labor agreement. A number of years ago, the parties had negotiated a provision that established a work schedule that was common for firefighters in many other communities in the region. The firefighters were split into four platoons, each working two days of ten hours each and then one day off, followed by two nights of fourteen hours each and then three days off. Thus, in a number of weeks, the firefighters worked forty-eight hours, and in other weeks they worked fewer hours. Over an eight-week cycle, all worked an average of forty-two hours per week.

Because of this schedule, firefighters had more time, and more opportunities, to obtain outside work or part-time jobs than did most other workers. Many of the firefighters held regular part-time jobs in the private sector or did moonlighting. There was no opposition to this kind of work agreement. In general, the fire chief was aware that many firefighters held jobs in the private sector, but this apparently did not affect the firefighters' performance and efficiency when working as a firefighter.

Prior to the start of negotiations for a new contract, the union held a meeting to provide negotiation guidelines to its negotiation committee. One member suggested that if the work schedule could be adjusted to provide more consecutive days off, their outside work opportunities would be enhanced. After some discussion, it was suggested that the negotiating team seek to change the schedule so that firefighters would work two days of ten hours each, then two nights of fourteen hours each, and then four days off. The membership supported this schedule change, and it was put on the union's list of proposals submitted to the city. In support of this proposal, the union argued that the change would cost the city nothing while it could increase the outside earning capacity of the firefighters.

Normally, negotiation sessions are kept off the record, with proposals and discussions kept away from the media. But a slip occurred somewhere, and the local press reported on a number of issues discussed in negotiations, including the union's proposed change in work schedule. The newspaper article noted that a substantial number of firefighters already held a second job, and the schedule change would permit a larger proportion of the firefighters to do so. This disclosure brought a flood of letters to the newspaper, severely criticizing the existing practice as well as the union proposal. A newspaper editorial that followed also blasted the firefighters' practice of holding a second job.

This public outcry put the city's negotiating team in a dilemma. It initially had looked favorably at the union proposal but now felt it could not grant the union this cost-free proposal. The public was too incensed over the idea of a public service employee's (a firefighter) holding a second job. The union battled hard at the negotiating table for this item, but to no avail. After numerous sessions, the parties reached a settlement for a two-year contract, with no change in the work schedule.

Discussion Issues, Problems, and Questions

1. In view of the existing work schedule, which gave firefighters three consecutive days off from work, what was wrong with a schedule giving firefighters four consecutive days off? (Keep in mind that the proposed change in no way affected the amount of time the firefighters worked for the city.) What concerned the public?
2. Had you been at the union meeting where the issue was proposed, would you have supported it? Why or why not?
3. If you were a city negotiator, would you have refused to accept the union proposal on work schedule? Why or why not? In view

of the fact that this union proposal was cost free to the city, could you have not gained other concessions by granting the union this proposal?
4. Could this type of problem have arisen in the private sector? If so, under what set of conditions?

Case 3: Cost of Medical Insurance

The city of Biltmore is located in a highly industrialized area in the Northeast and has a fire department of one hundred firefighters. There had been a collective bargaining relationship between the city and the firefighters' union for over thirty years. The private sector in this city had been largely organized for over forty years. In general, labor relations in Biltmore and in most of the surrounding cities and towns had been peaceful, with only an occasional brief strike.

Many years back, the firefighters' union had negotiated a provision in the contract that the city would pay 99 percent of the costs of medical insurance. At the time, this provision apparently did not seem excessive, in view of the various health hazards encountered in firefighting. As medical insurance costs began rising rather rapidly in the 1980s, the mayor of Biltmore surveyed the surrounding communities and found that all were paying 75 percent or less of medical insurance costs.

In the spring of 1984, when the parties began negotiating to replace the contract expiring on June 30, the city proposed that its share of the cost of health insurance be reduced from 99 percent to 75 percent. The city failed to achieve this change but did succeed in getting a provision that introduced a physical fitness program in which all firefighters had to participate "if needed." Many firefighters participated in the program, but many others did not, declaring that it was not needed.

In the spring of 1986, when the parties started negotiations for a new contract, the city again proposed a reduction of its share of costs of health insurance from 99 percent to 75 percent. The city again failed, but it succeeded in getting a provision that stipulated certain physical standards and required an annual physical fitness examination for all employees, at the city's expense. Some of the older firefighters indicated some opposition to this provision, but they apparently realized that some level of physical fitness was necessary to perform firefighting duties.

In the spring of 1988, at the start of negotiations, the city again proposed a reduction in its share of health insurance costs to 75 percent. It also submitted a proposal that all firefighters must give up smoking completely within one year of the signing of the labor agreement. The proposal to reduce the city's share of insurance costs again failed. On the no-smoking proposal, a compromise was worked out after long and hard bargaining: all new employees had to be nonsmokers who agreed never to smoke while employed as firefighters.

By the spring of 1990, a rather severe recession had hit the region, and the city was hard pressed financially. When the city went into negotiations, it again proposed a reduction of its share of insurance costs to 75 percent. It also included in its list of demands a no-smoking rule for all firefighters, effective at the signing of the labor agreement. Because of the grave financial situation, there was little money on the table for a wage increase. The negotiation sessions were long, bitter, and numerous, and the parties were still relatively far apart on a number of issues as the deadline of June 30 approached. Late in June, a breakthrough on a number of issues occurred, with tentative agreements on wages and some nonmonetary provisions, but the issues of reducing the city's share of health insurance costs and the no-smoking proposal were still unresolved. The city then said that unless it got one of these two proposals, with no modification, it would not settle on those matters that had already been tentatively agreed upon. The union now faced a dilemma. The contract expired June 30, and no new agreement was reached.

Discussion, Issues, Problems, and Questions

1. If you were a consultant to the city's negotiating team in 1990, would you have advised the city to take the position it did: demanding one or the other of the two remaining issues, without any modifications? If your answer is "yes," what do you think the advantages to the city are? If your answer is "no," what would you have advised? Explain your answer in detail.
2. If you were a consultant to the union's negotiating team, what

would you advise them to do? Would you want to have more information, and what kind, before giving advice? On what basis would you suggest that one alternative is better than the other for the union, as an ongoing organization?

3. If you were a nonsmoking union member, how would you vote on the alternative? If you were a smoking union member, how would you vote? What do you think would happen to the union if half of the members were smokers, and the union agreed to a nonsmoking provision in its labor agreement? Should the city mayor and other administrators be concerned about an issue that could split apart the firefighters' union?

4. If you were selected as the impartial arbitrator to arbitrate only these two issues, what would your decision be? What explanation would you give as to how and why you arrived at your decision? Would you consider giving the city part of both proposals? How would you do it? What would be the advantages and disadvantages of such an approach?

Case 4: Roll Call Time

The town of Upsula had grown very rapidly since 1980, with some industrialization from the overflow of neighboring cities. By 1988 it had a police force of seventy-five officers who formed a union that was recognized by the town as the bargaining agent. Following the pattern of labor agreements of police officers in comparable communities, the town and the union negotiated their first contract with few problems. The duration was for two years, from July 1, 1988, to June 30, 1990.

The chief of police had been a police officer in Upsala, had been promoted up the ranks, and had been appointed chief in 1980. He knew many of the officers personally and was considered to be fair and capable. He had always followed the town's historical practice of roll call at the start of each shift. All officers came in for roll call ten minutes before the shift, according to a regulation issued by the chief many years earlier.

When the first contract was signed, a provision set the hours for each shift, with time and one-half to be paid for all times on duty outside shift hours; no reference was made in the labor agreement to roll call time, but the past practice was confirmed. However, under the agreement, the officers were paid time and one-half their regular rate for the ten minutes of roll call time.

In the spring of 1989, the police chief's son-in-law, a police officer on the 7:00 A.M. to 3:00 P.M. shift, got a part-time job in the private sector that made it impossible for him to get to the police station before 7:00 A.M. Both the chief and many other officers knew that some officers had part-time jobs in the private sector, but there was never a conflict with the hours of the police requirements. The son-in-law failed to show at roll call many times, and sometimes he failed to arrive on time at the start of the shift at 7:00 A.M.

Early in September, the police chief issued a new regulation, effective October 1, 1989, that roll call would be held ten minutes after the shift instead of ten minutes before the start of it. This regulation did not violate the labor agreement, and the officers agreed that this change in rules was within the chief's prerogative. Many officers, however, were annoyed that their schedules were upset for the convenience of the chief's son-in-law.

In spring 1990, when the parties met to negotiate a new contract, to be effective July 1, 1990, the union submitted a list of demands that included a provision specifying a fifteen-minute roll call before the start of each shift. The police chief had not attended or participated in the negotiation sessions for the first contract in 1988 and was not in attendance at this first session in spring 1990. The negotiating team was composed of the mayor and three members of the town council. The members of the town negotiating team had heard about the police chief's change of roll call time and the reason for it, but they had not expected this to be an issue in the collective bargaining process. The mayor suggested that even preliminary discussion of this issue be delayed until the next bargaining session, when the chief would be invited to participate. The union agreed.

Having been briefed by the mayor about the union's proposal on roll call, the police chief attended the next bargaining session with a survey of police contracts of neighboring communities. When called upon to discuss the issue, he angrily charged the union with attempting to undermine his authority and noted that all but one of ten police labor contracts in neighboring communities were silent on the roll call issue, indicating that the police chief set the rules under his authority as chief. The mayor supported the police chief's position and indicated that the town strongly opposed the union's demands.

The union defended its demand; the chief had disregarded the interests of the vast majority of the officers and had made no effort to discuss the possible change in roll call time with the union or any other member of the police force. And with reference to proposing an increase to fifteen minutes for roll call, the union noted that the most common practice was a fifteen-minute roll call.

Although there were many other issues, including a wage adjustment, on the bargaining table, none of the others generated as much heat and anger as the roll call issue. The parties gradually whittled down their differences on many issues proposed by the union and the city, but neither was willing to compromise on roll call.

Discussion Issues, Problems, and Questions

1. There was no question that the police chief had the authority to change the roll call from the start of the shift to the end of it. If no provision of the labor agreement was violated by this change, what right did the union have to complain? Did the chief have an obligation to confer with the union before using his managerial authority to make the change? Was his action arbitrary and capricious, when he acted solely for the convenience of his son-in-law?

2. What was the union's motive in proposing an increase in roll call time from ten to fifteen minutes? Do you think the union had a chance of winning these extra five minutes, paid for at time and one-half? If you were a union leader, would you be willing to give up the extra five minutes of roll call time if the chief reversed his position and set roll call time at the start of the shift? Or would you be willing to give up your demand for roll call at the start of the shift in order to get the extra five minutes?

3. If you were the impartial arbitrator on this one issue, how would you resolve it? In view of the fact that the issue arose as a non-monetary problem (the authority of the chief and his arbitrary action), would you permit the money aspect (the proposed change from ten minutes to fifteen minutes) to be a bargaining wedge?

6

Resolution of Disputes

A whole range of disputes occurs in the public sector between employer and union, as they do in the private sector. There are interest disputes, involving terms and conditions of employment, as well as rights disputes (grievances) over the meaning or application of the terms of an existing agreement. Many of the disputes are over the same issues in both sectors, but the means and measures open to the parties in the public sector to resolve these disputes are different.

In interest disputes, the key difference in the settlement procedures between the public and the private sectors is the general right to strike by unions in the private sector. Collective bargaining and the settlement of interest disputes in the public sector generally try to copy the private sector model of negotiation and mediation, but without the next private sector step of the strike. The rationale for this limitation on labor organizations in the public sector had included the arguments of sovereignty of government, the essential services performed by government employees, and the noncompetitive monopolies of government services compared to free market prices in the private sector. Thus, in interest disputes, the settlement procedures differ between the public and private sectors. However, in disputes involving rights, the process of settlement through arbitration is basically the same in both sectors.

In the process of collective bargaining, the theoretical resolution of disputes depends on the relative bargaining power of the two parties within a framework of law. There are, however, no universal determinants of bargaining power. The skill of the bargainers as well as institutional, political, economic, and legal factors have an impact. In general, public policies affecting labor relations over the past fifty years have focused on equalizing the bargaining power of employers and unions. In the public sector, policies have attempted to balance the right to bargain, generally without resort to strike or lockout, with the protection of management's interest, under the general assumption that management is the custodian of the public interest.[1] Nevertheless, there has not been a consistent public policy in regard to public employees. Conditions and attitudes change. In the early 1960s, for example, efforts were made to help public employees catch up to private sector conditions. More recently, efforts are being made to restrain further increases for public employees because of employer-taxpayer resistance as the economy shrinks, unemployment increases, and the tax base decreases.

This chapter explores the setting in which labor relations disputes occur in the public sector and the processes by which the parties to the disputes attempt to resolve them.

Collective Bargaining and Civil Service

The merit system, normally administered by a civil service commission, has a long history in the public sector. For many years prior to the advent of collective bargaining in the public sector, wages were set by the employer, and the civil service commission set out the rules of personnel administration. The commission was also the arbiter of disputes concerning its own rules and regulations. With the establishment of collective bargaining in the public sector, and wages and working conditions being set by negotiations, conflict between collective bargaining and the merit system was inevitable. If merit, as determined by the employer, was the basis of retention and promotion, would this be in direct conflict with a union's proposal of seniority as the basis for layoff and promotion? On many issues, collective bargaining has had an impact on the civil service rules and regulations.

The authority of the administrators of the merit system is threatened by collective bargaining since unions share in the decision making that heretofore was management's exclusive domain. Once collective bargaining is introduced in a public sector (whether federal, state, or local), there is potential conflict and friction with an entrenched civil service commission. Questions immediately arise as to who is to represent the employer for purposes of negotiations, particularly over operating rules of the workplace, and what will be the scope of the negotiations. Friction with the civil service commission also can exist in the administration of the labor agreement, for a traditional function of civil service is to provide public service employees with a structured procedure for interpreting and applying contract benefits and appealing discipline and discharge. In many situations, conflict is resolved by establishing an independent and parallel procedure. In some situations, a disciplined employee may resort to more than one appeals procedure, one after the other. Possible friction between the two systems is often avoided by the recognition that both systems do exist side by side.

If the civil service commission is pushed aside to some extent by the advent of unions and collective bargaining, who negotiates for the employer? In many jurisdictions there is a fragmented employer authority for bargaining, frequently with final approval of any resolution by the legislature. Management power in the public sector is different across different branches of government and public officials. Generally a tentative agreement requires approval of the elected public executive, such as the mayor or the governor. Funding for such agreements frequently requires approval of the appropriate legislative body, such as a city council or a state legislature. It may also be noted that public employers are ultimately responsible to an electorate, and public employees make up a large bloc of voters.[2]

The Negotiation Process

The initial efforts of employers and employee organizations to reach agreement on the terms and conditions of employment within a specific framework of law are commonly described as the process of negotiation. The parties meet and discuss the issues that each would like to see in or deleted from their collective bargaining agreement. If the parties are meeting to determine the terms of a first agreement, the issues are generally numerous, in an effort to cover all aspects of the working relationship. If the parties are meeting to make changes in an existing contract, there are fewer issues to be discussed.

Prior to the start of any negotiations, the parties have a number of administrative and procedural matters to determine. One of the critical matters is the composition of each of the negotiating teams. Who makes up each of the teams, and what is the authority of the negotiators? What are the limits of the employer team, compared to the executive or legislature of the community? What is the timing of the negotiations? Should negotiations begin before or after the funding dates? What limits does the budget have on the authority of the negotiators and the timing of the negotiations? Matters such as these may have a significant impact on the whole process of negotiations.

The negotiation process itself involves the parties' meeting, exchanging proposals, and discussing the various items in the proposals. In some instances, the parties may quickly agree on a specific provision, while disagreeing strongly over another one. Based on arguments and data supporting a position such as comparability, the CPI, or ability to pay, the other party may shift its position slightly or significantly. There is a constant give and take, with concessions being made by one party in response to concessions by the other within an overall concept of an agreement by each side. The principle of settlement by negotiation is that generally the respective positions of the parties move closer together, until all open issues are resolved. In the private sector, there is always the possible threat of a strike. In the public sector, with few exceptions, no strikes are allowed, and with no deadlines, negotiations may drag on.

Depending on the specific issues and the number involved, negotiations may move smoothly, or they may go on over a period of months without total resolution. When negotiations are protracted, one side or the other may threaten to break off the talks without a final resolution. In most situations when a breakdown in negotiations appears imminent, the parties are likely to call in an outsider, a professional mediator, to assist the parties in reaching a settlement. In most public sector (nonfederal) situations, the mediator is an employee of a state agency. The federal government provides limited service in public sector mediation. In some instances the parties may agree on a private person to mediate or on a continuing umpire.

The Mediation Process

The mediation process has generally been described as the intercession of an impartial person in a dispute for the purpose of assisting the disputing parties to resolve their differences voluntarily. The goal of the outsider is to help the parties reach an agreement on their own. Labor mediation is one of the most highly institutionalized methods of resolving conflicts and is generally the starting point for statutory impasse procedures in the private or public sector.

Mediation in the private sector, where labor disputants agree on the use of an impartial third person to help the parties resolve a specific problem in impasse, has a long history. As far back as 1913, the U.S. Conciliation Service supplied staff mediators in certain private sector disputes. With the passage of the National Labor Relations Act in 1935 and the Labor-Management Relations Act (LMRA) in 1947, the collective bargaining process in the private sector became well established. To help the parties resolve bargaining impasses, the federal government in the LMRA established the Federal Mediation and Conciliation Service (FMCS) as an independent agency with jurisdiction primarily in disputes in the private sector, as well as those involving federal employees.[3] Mediation is the least intrusive of all efforts by outsiders to resolve disputes and is probably the most commonly used procedure in dispute resolution.

Two other federal agencies also provide mediation services, but in specialized sectors. The National Mediation Board provides services to certain types of labor disputes in the railroad and airline industries, and the Atomic Energy Labor Relations Panel, now associated with FMCS, provides mediation service in disputes in atomic energy plants. Many of the states that have passed legislation authorizing collective bargaining by state employees and local community employees have established agencies that provide mediation services to these public employees. Thus, in both the private and the public sectors, the vast majority of mediation services is provided by the employees of public agencies (federal and state), while others hire private mediators. Private labor arbitrators who may have had some mediation experience with a public agency or whose experience in arbitration appears to give them special expertise may be called in by the parties to a labor dispute to serve as mediator. In some special cases, a nonprofessional mediator such as a mayor of a city, a legal scholar, or clergy may be called in by the parties to help them resolve their differences.

The mediator's role is to assist the parties in a dispute to reach a resolution to their impasse, but there are different views as to how the process functions and what the qualifications are for a successful mediator. Depending on the experience of the mediator as well as his or her personality and view of the problems facing the parties and the mediator's relations with the parties, the process of mediation may vary. And the success of the mediator may be determined not only by his or her personality and experience in that sector but by his or her ability to size up the parties, their relative power, their positions, and their minimum requirements and to persuade and cajole the parties into a compromise. A mediator can approach the situation in a variety of ways:[4]

- By controlling the flow of information between the parties.
- By developing mutually acceptable factual data to provide a setting for the discussion of a particular issue.
- By serving as a private, informal adviser to each side in the development of settlement package proposals.
- By developing distinctive settlement packages different from those put forth by the parties.
- By exerting moral authority or reflection of a public interest in the resolution of a dispute.

Mediation, on the whole, is successful, especially considering the fact that it is a technique without power. The FMCS reports that it settles approximately 80 percent of all impasses it is asked to mediate, and in most states the settlement rate is close to this average.[5]

There has been a shift into a combination of the mediation process and interest arbitration—that is, arbitration of the terms of a labor agreement. It has long been a custom to use mediation as the first step in resolving a dispute over the terms of a new labor agreement; however, this mediation was generally performed by a federal or state mediator, and if the process failed to resolve the dispute, the mediator withdrew from the situation. If at this point, or later, the parties agreed to arbitrate their dispute, an arbitrator would then be selected to arbitrate the unresolved issues. In a merger of these two processes, a person is selected to mediate and, if necessary, arbitrate the unresolved issues. The mediator helps the parties reach an agreement on their own; the arbitrator issues a final and binding award.

The Strike as an Alternative

In the private sector, the use of an arbitrator to determine the terms of a labor contract is still relatively rare. For various reasons, the parties to a labor dispute generally do not view an arbitrator's determination of the terms and condition of employment as acceptable and generally prefer to exert economic power than hand the determination of their collective bargaining agreement to an outsider. The ultimate economic weapon is the strike (or lockout), which is designed to exert economic pressure by depriving the other party of revenues or employment. The parties are often up against a deadline, set by the termination date of the existing contract. If the terms of a new contract are not reached, a strike or lockout may occur. A strike may prove to be a fragile situation, since either side could close down the company permanently.

In the public sector, the strike has a fundamentally different effect. Here, its principal purpose is to exert political pressure on public officials and to deprive some members of the public of some type of service. Management is not deprived of revenues, but it may lose political support of those who are inconvenienced by the disruption of service. In some cases, however, the public has supported a hard line taken by management against a public employee stoppage.[6]

The question whether a collective bargaining impasse in the public sector should be settled by arbitration or by a work stoppage is unresolved. Although the strike is prohibited in the federal sector and is considered a felony, the arbitration of impasses is not mandated. Despite being illegal in all but ten states, strikes by public sector employees do occur throughout the country. In these ten states, there is not total freedom to strike; strikes by public safety employees are still prohibited. According to one study from the 1960s to the 1980s, the number of strikes increased drastically, until one of every eight in 1979 and 1980 occurred in the public sector; these strikes, however, were generally of short duration. Yet despite the increase in illegal strikes, the vast majority of collective bargaining agreements in the public sector were reached through negotiations between the parties, without resource to arbitration or to the strike. One study suggests that when the parties are given the choice of arbitration or strike, their ability to reach a negotiated settlement is higher than would normally be expected under a simple arbitration system; at the same time, the incidence of work stoppages is substantially lower than the strike rates reported for simple strike systems.[7]

Although there are different findings on the incidence and impact of strikes in the public sector, the following conclusions are generally accepted:

• Interest arbitration has been successful in reducing strike activity. Strikes are most likely to occur in states without a bargaining law that provides some form of interest arbitration.
• Strike penalties, when they are enforced, can deter strikes.
• State policies other than collective bargaining policies can have an important impact on strike activity.[8]

In the federal sector, the recent tone of policy with respect to the strike was set in 1981 by President Reagan's handling of the strike by air traffic controllers. The Professional Air Traffic Controllers Organization (PATCO), representing 17,000 air traffic controllers from 1972 to 1981, went out on strike in August 1981. Under federal law the strike was illegal. Most of the strikers ignored a presidential back-to-work order and were fired. PATCO was decertified, and this meant the dissolution of the union. Controllers who had gone out on strike were refused reemployment. The harshness of the government reaction in this case put a danger on possible strike activity by other federal employees.

Previously, the federal government had reacted significantly differently to federal employee strikes. For example, the 1972 U.S. Postal Service Employees' strike was a felony, and all strikers should have been fired. They were not. The government privatized the Postal Service under the Postal Reorganization Act, and the employees then came under the labor laws relevant to the private sector.

Strikes, stoppages, and slowdowns by public employees continue to occur in state and local communities, despite their illegality (although there appears to have been a decline in such activity since 1981): teachers go out on strike; garbage collectors slow down; transit workers work by the rules and slow down the system; firefighters engage in a "sick-out"; and police are stricken by the blue flu or fail to hand out traffic and parking citations. Whether a strike is an outright violation of the law or clear subversion of it, strike penalties are often difficult to enforce. A community cannot fire all police, or firefighters, or teachers. The union is likely to make the removal of penalties a precondition for a settlement of the dispute, and management is likely to agree in order to restore service as quickly as possible. The resort to interest arbitration has probably lessened the incidence of public sector strikes. However, in view of the variations among states and communities in labor relations policies and in approaches to the settlement of public sector disputes, there will likely continue to be some strikes, stoppages, and slowdowns in the public sector.

Fact-Finding and Arbitration

Despite the illegality of the strike in most public sector jurisdictions, public sector unions and managements do not readily accept final and binding arbitration as a substitute for the strike. Most unions, both public and private, show some resistance to turning over the determination of the terms and conditions of employment to an outside neutral party. Many feel they are likely to do better through direct negotiations with employers or through the economic pressure of a strike or slowdown. However, they also tend to accept binding arbitration, reluctantly, because they have more to lose by an impasse. Public employers also show resistance to the arbitration process, arguing that it means the surrender of their public authority and responsibility to an outsider who is not responsive to the electorate, usurps their legislative function, and does not take into account the community's willingness to pay. Nevertheless, about twenty states have given arbitrators the responsibility for settling disputes involving the terms of employment when the public employer and the union cannot resolve their differences, although in some states arbitration awards are subject to legislature approval of funding.

There is an intermediate step that many state legislatures find acceptable before resort to a strike or lockout: fact-finding, a nonbinding procedure. Here, an outside neutral, a fact finder, is selected or designated by a state agency to hold a fact-finding hearing where each side has an opportunity of presenting the facts and its arguments on all of the issues involved in the dispute. Occasionally, the fact finder engages in mediation, and frequently, posthearing briefs to summarize the parties' respective positions and legal arguments are filed by the parties. The fact finder issues findings and recommendations on each of the issues involved, but they are not binding on the parties. The goal of the process is for these recommendations to become the basis for further negotiations and a narrowing of the differences between the parties. In many situations, the recommendations of the fact finder form the basis for a settlement. Generally the purpose of fact-finding is to put public pressure on the parties to accept the recommendations. Parties often delay serious negotiations until after full-time mediation and then the receipt of the fact finder's recommendations. Since the process lacks finality, many parties view it as an additional step required to get to the procedure that does have finality: arbitration.

Despite the finality of the arbitration process, there appear to be many problems with it in the public sector. State laws mandating interest arbitration for public employees have been challenged in the courts on constitutional grounds involving either the relationship of state to local authority or the relationship of arbitration to the legislative process. Some challenges stem from the provisions in state constitutions that prohibit the legislature from delegating to a special or private body any power to interfere with "municipal moneys or to perform municipal functions."[9] Although an increasing number of state courts have upheld the constitutionality of interest arbitration, there still remain some problems.

The rules governing binding arbitration differ among jurisdictions. It may be mandated for only police and firefighters, it is permissible for police and firefighters, or permissible for all public employees, or there may be no statute provisions on the subject. When the law is silent on the matter, is it permissible for a public sector union to demand binding arbitration to resolve its dispute over a contract? And if the law is silent, may the parties voluntarily agree to binding arbitration in an interest impasse? These are problems that have not been resolved across the nation.

Where arbitration is permissible or mandatory, there still remain problems as to which issues are arbitrable or prohibited from arbitration, as well as the role of the courts in resolving such matters. Once arbitration awards are handed down, what role do the courts play in reviewing these awards? There is no simple answer to this question. Rather, there is variation from state to state, and sometimes within a state, over the issues in the award. Legislatures and courts have held that certain issues are not arbitrable under any circumstance, and courts have overruled arbitration awards where they have found that an arbitrator has exceeded his or her jurisdiction. Recently, there have been a growing number of court decisions overruling arbitration awards that are held to be directing or condoning a breach of law or public policy.

Many state laws or regulations spell out the factors that are to be given weight by arbitrators in arriving at interest arbitration awards. On economic issues, the most common ones include the following:

(1) The financial ability of the municipality to meet costs.

(2) The interests and welfare of the public.

(3) The hazards of employment, physical, educational, and mental qualifications, job training and skills involved.

(4) A comparison of wages, hours, and conditions of employment . . . with . . . other employees performing similar services and with other employees generally in public or private employment, in comparable communities.

(5) The decisions and recommendations of the fact-finder, if any.

(6) The average consumer prices for goods and services, commonly known as the cost of living.

(7) The overall compensation presently received by the employees, including direct wages and fringe benefits.

(8) Changes in any of the foregoing circumstances during the pendency of the arbitration proceeding.

(9) Such other factors . . . which are normally or traditionally taken into consideration in . . . voluntary collective bargaining, mediation, fact-finding, or arbitration. . . .

(10) The stipulation of the parties.[10]

In the public sector the public employer's ability to pay is a special consideration. As an increasing number of states have adopted cap laws that limit spending by some formula or percentage, the arbitration standard of ability to pay looms more important. If a community is limited on its expenditures in some fashion by a state law, arbitrators cannot casually disregard such limits. But are arbitrators qualified to weigh the costs of an award against tax increases and other competing public expenditures, some of which may be mandated by law? Should arbitrators substitute their judgment in issuing an award for the judgment of elected officials? There are no easy answers to these questions. Unions may argue that arbitrators should use comparability data as their major guideline, giving little, if any, weight to the argument of inability to pay. Public employers may argue that they have a public responsibility to all groups and services of the community and that when they make an inability-to-pay argument, arbitrators should seriously consider it without giving excessive weight to comparability data. Arbitrators are frequently placed in the center of such a dilemma: they are confined to a single segment of the public sector yet must consider the impact of any award on both the overall mission of the community and the interests of other employees. According to one labor arbitrator, there is a more basic dilemma:

> The final dilemma of interest arbitration in the public sector—perhaps its ultimate dilemma—is this: if the interest arbitrator performs his assignment so wisely, skillfully, and imaginatively that the parties eventually come to prefer arbitration of their disputes to face-to-face bargaining, an arbitrator would have undermined the system of free collective bargaining that gave life to his role and that he has pledged to serve. On the other hand, if he performs unwisely, crudely, and unimaginatively to the general dissatisfaction of the parties, they would have been encouraged to return to free collective bargaining and redouble their efforts at private settlement so as to escape the scourge of compulsory arbitration.[11]

The form of interest arbitration may have some impact on the outcome of the arbitration award. In most arbitration proceedings, a single neutral arbitrator, selected by the parties or appointed by a prescribed selection process, presides. In other proceedings, there are tripartite arbitration boards in which the chair, a neutral arbitrator, is selected jointly by the parties, with each side appointing a representative to sit with the neutral arbitrator. In this form, decisions are based on a majority vote, making it incumbent on the chair to convince the labor representative or the employer representative, or both, to vote with him or her on the award. In other localities, the representatives of the parties may act only as advisers to the arbitrator. The form of the arbitration panel is sometimes prescribed by law, but often the parties determine the form.

There are two basic kinds of interest arbitration: conventional arbitration and final-offer arbitration. In conventional arbitration, the arbitrator, or the arbitration panel, may select the position of either party or fashion a compromise on any single issue or among the issues in dispute. Final-offer arbitration was devised as a variant to the traditional arbitration in an effort to put additional pressure on the parties to reach an agreement. As initially conceived, final-offer arbitration was an all-or-nothing process; the arbitrator selected the total package of proposals by the union or that by the employer, with no authority to compromise any position or to select the position of one party on one issue and the other party's position on another issue. But over the years, a number of variations of final-offer arbitration have been devised. The principal variant is final offer, issue by issue, under which the arbitrator may select the position of either party on an issue-by-issue basis. In some states, arbitrators may also select, on an issue-by-issue basis, from the recommendations made by a fact finder, thereby giving the arbitrator a choice from three positions on each issue. Other variations exist as well. Under a New Jersey law that applies to police and firefighter contract disputes, the parties can select conventional arbitration, a variety of final-offer techniques, or any other solution; if they fail to agree on a process, they must use final-offer arbitration, treating all economic items as a package and noneconomic issues on an issue-by-issue basis.[12]

Most states that authorize collective bargaining for some of their public employees also provide some type of arbitration for at least police and firefighters. About half of the states provide for conventional arbitration and the others for some variation of final-offer arbitration. Despite the availability of arbitration, the vast majority of public sector negotiations in those states were resolved without resort to the arbitration process. Some researchers believe that arbitration has a narcotic effect; once the parties resort to arbitration, they will become dependent on it for settling all future disputes. Others argue that arbitration chills negotiations because the parties know that their compromise may be expanded by the arbitrator. The internal politics of each group undoubtedly is a factor in favoring arbitration or direct negotiations. Research indicates that in states where arbitration is available for public sector employees, it is used in from 10 to 15 percent of the negotiations covered by the statute.[13]

The merits of conventional arbitration versus final-offer arbitration have been debated, without a clear answer that one is better. When only one issue is involved, there is little difference between the two. When a number of issues are involved, the conventional arbitration process gives the arbitrator the opportunity to fashion an award that is, from the arbitrator's perspective, equitable to both parties; but the award is frequently viewed by the parties as a compromise between positions on an issue or as a trade-off on issues. The final-offer arbitration process puts a premium on each party's ability to fashion a final offer that will win the arbitrator's selection. The arbitrator may dislike each party's proposals but must select one. Arbitrators have questioned the effects of such awards on the long-run labor relations of the parties.

A Special Case

Each state has its own specific laws covering collective bargaining for public sector employees, and many provide for arbitration of negotiating impasses, especially for police and firefighters. A detailed study of some of these state procedures was published in 1984.[14] Here, we look at a relatively unique process that was developed in Massachusetts.

In 1964 the Massachusetts legislature gave state employees the right to organize and to bargain collectively, and in the following year, legislation was passed requiring municipal, county, and public school employers to bargain with employee organizations certified as majority representatives by a state labor relations commission. The Board of Conciliation and Arbitration, which already had mediation responsibility in both the private and public sectors, was given responsibility for overseeing fact-finding in the public sector.

There was no provision for a final resolution of an impasse, and the use of the strike or lockout was prohibited.

Effective July 1, 1974, Massachusetts provided a mechanism for final resolution of disputes over the terms of collective agreements for police and firefighters in cities and towns of the state.[15] Case 5 of this chapter discusses this mechanism. The mechanism provided was last-best-offer arbitration after fact-finding with recommendations. Initially the arbitrator was required to choose between the package of final proposals made by the union and that made by the employer; this was later changed so that the arbitrator could also elect the package of recommendations made by the fact finder. The arbitrator's award was binding on both parties and the municipal legislative body, which was required to appropriate the funds.

During the three-year period 1974–1977, approximately one hundred last-best-offer arbitration awards were issued, and the management organizations for the cities and towns became convinced that the process favored the police and fire unions. When the statute was renewed in June 1977 for another two years, representatives of the cities and towns and of the firefighters' union approached John T. Dunlop of Harvard University to help resolve the controversy. He fashioned an agreement between the parties in September, and the contents were enacted into law on November 15. The major police organization had been kept advised of the developments and joined in the resulting agency, the Joint Labor-Management Committee for Police and Fire (JLMC), which was to begin handling cases on January 1, 1978.

The statute establishing the JLMC provided for a committee of six representatives of cities and towns (such as mayors, city managers, or selectmen), three representatives of municipal police, three representatives of firefighters, and a neutral chair (and later a vice-chair). The governor appoints the nominees of the organizations. The committee members from labor and management serve without compensation; the chair and vice-chair are paid on a per-diem basis for days worked. Throughout most of its operation, the committee has had a staff of three investigators/mediators, a senior labor and a senior management staff person who work as a team, a fiscal administrative officer, and a secretary. The JLMC has broad oversight responsibility for all collective bargaining negotiations involving Massachusetts municipal police officers and firefighters.

It uses a variety of tools and mechanisms in the resolution of disputes: staff mediation, senior staff, committee members, neutrals on the committee, special outside representatives, fact-finding with insiders or outsiders, limited arbitration with insiders or outsiders, or a combination of these methods. The committee meets regularly (at least once a month) to review every pending case, to hear reports and review developments, to design procedures appropriate to cases at their current stage, and to take formal actions to report to the parties. Virtually every action it has taken, procedural or substantive, has been by a unanimous vote. By statute, the JLMC also serves as a forum for the discussion of current issues in public safety labor-management relations and strives to foster an environment conducive to responsible collective bargaining.

Since 1978, the authority of the JLMC with respect to arbitration has changed. Initially it had the authority to order last-best-offer arbitration, with insiders or outsiders as arbitrators. Such arbitration awards were binding on the executive and legislative bodies of the community involved. In November 1980, a statewide referendum was approved that imposed a limit on state and local taxes on real estate and personal property equal to 2 ½ percent of its full and fair cash value. The referendum question also included the elimination of the provision of the state law for compulsory, last-best-offer arbitration in municipal and police and firefighter negotiations. On February 10, 1981, the attorney-general of Massachusetts issued an advisory opinion holding that the JLMC continued to have authority to order final and binding arbitration on the executive officers of a community but not on a legislative body requiring it to appropriate the requisite funds. Despite this opinion, the JLMC elected not to order an executive to arbitrate, choosing extended and often protracted mediation and fact-finding when necessary. Without the use of a process with finality, a growing number of cases remained unsettled for extended periods of times.

Despite the difficulties of settlement due to the lack of a procedure with finality, cases were settled, without work stoppages by strike or lockout. The small staff of mediators, aided by management and union representatives of the JLMC, managed to resolve the vast majority of contract disputes using a range of techniques from plain mediation to fact-finding to "advisory recommendations." However, the time needed to settle disputes grew, and the tension among the parties grew sharper.

At the initiation of members of the JLMC, a legislative commission was established to hold hearings on the situation. On December 21, 1987, the state legislature enacted Chapter 589 of the Acts of 1987, and section 3(a) authorized procedures for the JLMC to invoke limited arbitration. Under this authority, an arbitration award would be binding on the executive of a city or town but not on its legislative body in cases involving the appropriation of funds. Case 4 addresses this issue. The sunset provision included in section 3(a) was eliminated on March 30, 1990.

Although the JLMC's arbitration authority was limited, its existence had a salutary effect on contract negotiations involving police and firefighters. The time required to settle disputes did shorten, not because of a substantial use of arbitration but merely because of its existence and its potential use. In the three-year period from the enactment of Chapter 589 of 1987 to early 1991, the JLMC invoked the limited arbitration procedures in 4 cases out of more than 250 it handled in that period. (The appendix to this chapter contains the rules of the JLMC.)

The Resolution of Grievances

A grievance, in the lexicon of labor relations, is broadly defined as a complaint or a claim that the collective bargaining agreement has been violated or misapplied. The vast majority of labor contracts contain a grievance procedure that describes in varying degrees of detail the process and steps of resolving a grievance. Most such procedures provide binding arbitration as a final step in the process, as well as limits on the authority of the arbitrator.

The development of grievance procedures in private sector collective bargaining was well established before it was adopted in the public sector as a more economical and efficient way to resolve grievances than the previous avenue of strike. In the private sector it was a trade-off between the employer and the union where the union surrendered the strike right during the contract term and won protection against having to strike by the employer's commitment to abide by the arbitration award interpreting or applying the agreement. Following World War II, grievance procedures in private sector labor agreements became widespread, but in some cases, the grievance issue was appealed to the courts or enforcement of the award was sought by one party or the other. In 1960, in a series of decisions involving the United Steelworkers Union, commonly referred to as the steel-workers trilogy, the Supreme Court established arbitral finality so long as the award draws its essence from the labor contract.[16] One author summarized the rules laid down in these cases as follows:

(1) The role of the court is limited to determining whether the party seeking arbitration is making a claim which, on its face, is covered by the contract;
(2) The courts are not to consider the merits of a grievance under the guise of interpreting the arbitration clause of an agreement;
(3) In suits for performance of an arbitration agreement, arbitration should be ordered unless it is clear beyond doubt that the dispute is not covered by the contract's arbitration clause— doubts should be resolved in favor of coverage;
(4) An arbitrator's award is enforceable under Section 301 of the Taft-Hartley Act;
(5) In suits for enforcement of such awards, the courts may not overrule the arbitrator, simply because their interpretation of the contract is different from the arbitrators'.[17]

Over time, a growing number of state courts and state laws explicitly adopted the principle of arbitral finality as specified for the private sector by the Supreme Court.

Within the public sector there is considerable variation in the provisions for the resolution of grievances. Labor agreements affecting the post office, for example, are covered by the laws of the private sector, and grievances are handled in the same fashion as those in the private sector. All contain grievance procedures that terminate in binding arbitration.

Another variation involves public school teachers. Many state laws provide strong legislative rights for the employer not renewing non-tenured teachers, and for protection against termination of teachers who have served a three-year probationary period. Very few contracts surrender the employers' right to non renew non-tenured teachers. And even where arbitration is provided in tenure cases, arbitrators' jurisdiction is usually limited to procedural issues, with a rare grant of authority to determine just cause for removal. In some instances the award is not final and binding, thereby questioning whether the process is really arbitration. There often is available an administrative appeals procedure.

In the executive branch of the federal government arbitration is required as the final step in grievance procedures negotiated under the Civil Service Reform Act. However, relatively few grievances are arbitrable in the executive branch, partly due to the narrow scope of bargaining permitted in the federal government, as indicated in Chapter III. Those grievances that do reach the arbitration step are subject to numerous restrictions of law, rules and regulations, confining the arbitrators' authority, and when that is challenged they are open to greater review by the courts. Federal sector law subjects arbitration decisions to review by courts or administrative bodies, or both, to determine whether the arbitrators have exceeded their jurisdiction. This imposes new burdens on arbitrators to interpret external law and Federal rules and regulations, and in particular, limits arbitrators' ability to fashion appropriate remedies. The most common basis for exception to arbitration awards is the remedy, usually an award of back pay.[18] In recent years arbitrators have fashioned their awards with this problem in mind, and fewer awards have been set aside.

The process of grievance arbitration was slow to develop in state and local government, as was the right to collective bargaining. While the process was being used by teachers' organizations as early as the mid-1960's, there still appeared to be as late as the 1970's a marked reticence by state courts toward arbitral determination of some issues. Instances of court reticence arose where issues called for exercise of discretion not governed by explicit contract criteria, or where the award is seen as having potential impact upon the level or quality or service or upon financial resources.[19] By 1985 grievance arbitration was permitted or required in the public sector laws of a majority of states, and these laws generally gave public employees the right to negotiate grievance procedures and binding arbitration. A few states did require that labor agreements contain a grievance procedure capped by binding arbitration. Ten states* do not have public employee bargaining laws and grievance arbitration is prohibited. In these states management has nearly unfettered discretion with respect to the handling of grievance matters through their civil service laws, and the final step is the responsibility of an appointed commission rather than an outside arbitrator.[20]

The types of issues raised in grievance procedures are generally more limited in the public sector than in the private sector because the scope of the bargaining agreement is narrower; nevertheless, the issues in the public sector cover a wide range of questions and issues. According to one source, the most frequently arbitrated issues in state and local government between January 1983 to June 1985 and the number of occurrences were as follows:

Discipline and discharge, 315.
Arbitrability, 122.
Just cause, 84.
Management rights, 83.
Past practice, 70.
Overtime, 61.
Reinstatement and reimbursement from supervisor, 51.
Leaves of absence, 47.
Promotion, 47.
Union security, 46.
Disciplinary policies and procedures, 45.[21]

Although many of the same issues arise in both public and private sector arbitration, there are some differences. Discipline and discharge grievances in the public sector are often controlled by statute or civil service rules or are barred by contract language. Issues such as arbitrability and management rights involve the basic matter of the scope of collective bargaining, and because of the various limits on the scope of bargaining in the public sector, these issues arise more frequently in this sector. The frequency of other issues in the grievance procedures may vary to some degree from private to public sectors, but they may also vary widely among

---

* Arizona, Arkansas, Colorado, Louisiana, Mississippi, North Carolina, South Carolina, Utah, Virginia, and West Virginia.

units within each of the sectors. Promotion, for example, may become a frequent issue in bargaining units where promotion opportunities are many; where the employment structure is such that few promotion opportunities are available, the issue is of minor consequence.

Additionally, specific issues occur in a bargaining unit because of the nature of the work involved. A police bargaining unit, for example, may file a grievance over a rate for a private detail or the allocation of private detail work; a firefighter unit may grieve over a fire chief's order to paint fireplugs or the department's rule requiring firefighters to live in the community; and a teachers' bargaining unit may grieve over the size of a class for special students, lunchroom assignment duties during a "free period," or a requirement to attend faculty meetings after the end of the workday.

In some public sector situations, individual employees and unions are offered alternatives to arbitration and appeals routes from arbitration awards involving specific issues; employees may have a choice of procedures for their appeal, and if they lose in one forum, a second may also be open.[22] Some contracts or statutes offer a choice of routes, but not both, in some issues.

Grievance mediation is not a new process; it was rather common up to the 1940s in private sector labor relations, when disputes ended either in a strike or in mediation. During and after World War II, grievance arbitration became established as the final step in the grievance procedure. In 1947 the Taft-Hartley Act created the FMCS as an independent agency, and the act stated that the FMCS should not involve itself in resolving grievance disputes except in last-resort and exceptional cases. Many states employed full-time mediators for disputes over terms of a contract, and in a number of jurisdictions these mediators also became involved in the mediation of grievances.

The majority of professional work by labor arbitrators is arbitrating grievances, and the first reaction of many arbitrators to the intrusion of an intermediate step, mediation, was negative. Although some arbitrators have always engaged in efforts to mediate a grievance dispute, it was assumed, and still is by many arbitrators, that the mediation of a grievance is to be performed by someone other than the arbitrator. When the parties of a labor-management relationship adopt mediation as an intermediate stage prior to grievance arbitration the process frequently calls for a different professional (with perhaps different skills). When that fails, the arbitration process is invoked; however, where mediation succeeds, the arbitrator is eliminated from the process.

A growing number of arbitrators have made some effort to mediate grievances to which they have been assigned or selected to arbitrate. The form of mediation used by the grievance arbitrators may differ from the standard techniques, and some may question whether it is still mediation. If the arbitrator talks to both advocates simultaneously, is this mediation? There are no reliable figures as to the extent of such mediation efforts by arbitrators in grievance cases, but estimates indicate the number is small. Efforts appear to be most effective when the arbitrator knows the representatives of parties from previous cases or is named in the contract as the impartial arbitrator for grievances under the agreement. In such instances, there is a certain level of acceptability that may permit the arbitrator to try some form of mediation; if it fails, the arbitrator can revert to arbitration of the grievance. Success in mediating grievances shortens the time in resolving the grievance and also cuts the costs involved. Apparently many arbitrators feel that if they have been selected through the procedures of the American Arbitration Association or of the FMCS to arbitrate a specific grievance for specific parties, they have no right to attempt to mediate the dispute; they feel obligated to arbitrate the grievance, a procedure requested by the parties to the dispute. Furthermore, many arbitrators, whose sole experience has been the arbitration of grievances, feel unqualified to attempt to mediate a dispute.

Questions for Discussion

1. What are the major factors that make the resolution of labor disputes in the public sector more complex and more difficult than the private sector? Which factor do you consider the most significant, and why?

2. Why have civil service rules and procedures not made unions and collective bargaining unnecessary in the public sector? Would a single set of civil service rules and regulations for fed-

eral, state, and local community employers help to resolve labor disputes without unions and collective bargaining?

3. If the collective bargaining process has worked so well in the private sector, why has it not completely replaced the civil service system in the public sector? Where collective bargaining has replaced civil service in public sector labor disputes, who is the employer, who negotiates over the dispute, and who finally signs an agreement?

4. Why are there relatively few grievance arbitration cases in the federal government? Could this same system be imposed on the private sector in order to reduce grievances? Why or why not?

5. In states where grievance arbitration is prohibited, grievances are probably settled by some process. Do you think that employees with grievances are better served by arbitration or some other process? Explain your answer.

6. Why is mediation the most commonly used process to resolve disputes over the terms of a labor contract? Inasmuch as there is no finality in the mediation process, why is it considered highly successful?

7. In almost all units of the public sector, the strike is illegal. Without the strike or threat of a strike as a weapon, how do public sector unions manage to gain higher wages and improved benefits? What tactics do some public sector unions use as a substitute for the illegal strike?

8. Fact-finding offers recommendations but not finality in a labor dispute. Nevertheless, it has been successful in resolving disputes over labor contracts in many situations. How do you account for this success?

9. What are the advantages and disadvantages of conventional arbitration versus last-best-offer arbitration? In your opinion, which form of arbitration would a labor arbitrator prefer? Why? Under what conditions would an experienced lawyer prefer last-best-offer arbitration? Why? What are the advantages of a last-best-offer total package versus last-best-offer item by item?

10. What are the relatively unique features of the Massachusetts Joint Labor-Management Committee that have resulted in its success in the resolution of labor contract disputes between

Massachusetts communities and their police and firefighter bargaining units? How would you measure success?

Case 1: Seniority in Promotions

The secretarial and clerical employees of a state bureau are organized by a local of the American Federation of State, County, and Municipal Employees, and the parties have negotiated a collective bargaining agreement that contains a standard grievance procedure provision. Relevant here is a promotion provision that requires the employer to post all vacancies and permits employees to bid on these vacancies. Promotions are to be based on qualifications, skill, and ability; where skill and ability among applicants are relatively equal, the most senior of the applicants is to get the promotion.

The vast majority of members of the bargaining unit are women. There has been practically no turnover among the staff, and therefore no promotion jobs have been posted for over three years. Two years ago, due to an increase in work load, two additional clerk-typists were hired from the outside; one of the newly hired was a male.

When a secretary of the unit announced that she would be leaving for personal reasons, the secretarial vacancy was posted. Four clerk-typists filed for the posted vacancy: three females and the male clerk-typist hired two years ago. All of the secretarial positions were filled by females. All four applicants were interviewed and their personnel files reviewed by an administrative committee of the employer, as provided in the agreement. All three members of the administrative committee were males. The applicant selected for the promotion was the most senior of the applicants and was a female. The male applicant filed a grievance, contending he was the most qualified applicant.

Both the union shop steward and the business agent were women. They attended each step of the grievance procedure with the grievant but permitted him to present his case to the management representative. He based his case primarily on the fact that he was a college graduate and had three years of secretarial experience in the army. He also alleged he was being discriminated against because he was a male; all the managers were male, and they preferred a female secretary.

The grievance moved through the procedure without resolution, and the union was then faced with the question of whether to take the matter to arbitration. At a union meeting, many members argued that the woman selected for the promotion was qualified, competent, and the most senior applicant for the job, and therefore the union should not take the case to arbitration. Some male members argued that not taking the matter to arbitration was discriminatory and that the union could be sued for failure of fair representation, whereby a union is found by the courts not to have represented all members in an equal fashion. This was a telling argument, and by a bare majority, the union voted to send the case to arbitration.

Pursuant to the procedures outlined in the agreement, an arbitrator was selected and a hearing was held. Posthearing briefs were filed with the arbitrator, and the arbitrator then handed down her award. The award denied the grievance and held that the grievant's failure to be promoted did not violate the collective bargaining agreement.

The grievant immediately filed a petition with the state civil service commission, contending he was the most qualified applicant for the promotion but nevertheless was not granted the promotion in violation of civil service rules. After some preliminary investigation, the civil service held a hearing on the matter and then held that civil service rules were not violated when the grievant failed to get the promotion. By this time, eighteen months had passed since the original selection of the applicant for the promotion.

Turned down by the civil service commission, the grievant then filed a charge with the state's commission against discrimination, charging that his agency discriminated against him for the promotion because he was a male. Hearings were held by the commission and the decision handed down held that the commission did not find discrimination in the failure to promote the grievant. An additional year had elapsed.

The grievant had one more option: to take the matter to court.

Discussion Issues, Problems, and Questions

1. Do you think the grievant should have gotten the promotion?
2. Do you feel there was sex discrimination in the agency? Explain your answer.

3. Should the union have taken the case to arbitration? Why or why not? How much weight should be given to the argument of fair representation? Had the grievant been female, would the union have faced a tough problem of one member's vying with another over a promotion? Should the union always support the most senior member?
4. How many opportunities should the grievant have to press his claim? After being turned down by a labor arbitrator, should he have the right to another hearing in a different forum (such as the civil service commission)?
5. Would you be in favor of a provision in the grievance procedure of the collective bargaining agreement that reads as follows: "Any matter which is subject to the jurisdiction of the Civil Service Commission shall not be a subject of grievance or arbitration hereunder"? Why or why not?

Case 2: Unemployment and Budgets Affect a Settlement

The small town of Upsala has had a collective bargaining relationship with its maintenance employees, responsible for maintaining and repairing all public buildings, for over twenty years. The town is contiguous to a larger industrial city, and most of the residents are blue-collar semiskilled and unskilled workers who work in the larger city. All ten of the town's maintenance workers live in the town. The state law prohibits strikes of public employees but does permit collective bargaining. Through a state board of mediation, services are provided; there are no provisions for fact-finding or for arbitration.

The relationship between the town's mayor and council and the union's leadership has been relatively good. They apparently trust each other, and negotiations over new contracts are generally brief. The settlements reached in the past were based on the town's ability to pay and what some of the neighboring committees were paying. The parties regularly negotiated one-year agreements, commencing July 1.

A recession hit the area shortly before negotiations started for the contract that was to be effective July 1, 1989, and unemployment among the town's residents was about 8 percent. Other surrounding communities were also hit by unemployment, but none seemed as hard hit as Upsala. Because of fiscal constraints, as well as the general pessimism of the residents due to unemployment, the parties failed to reach an agreement after four negotiation sessions. For the first time, a mediator from the board of mediation was called in, and three more sessions were held with the mediator. The settlement reached provided a wage increase slightly below that of the average settlement in the neighboring communities. There was some resentment by a few union members at the settlement.

In the local elections in November 1989, a new mayor and a new town council were elected. There was no indication that the wage settlement with the union was an issue in any way. In September 1990, the union held its biannual elections and elected a new president. Here there was no doubt that the wage settlement was an issue; a member who had strongly opposed the July 1989 wage settlement was elected by a slight majority.

Negotiations for a new contract began in April 1991, and it was clear from the start that the new mayor and the new union president rubbed each other the wrong way. The recession had deepened, and unemployment in Upsala had jumped to 11 percent. The union argued that wages and benefits were well behind those of comparable communities and that Upsala had fallen further behind the others, and it proposed a 3 percent increase in wages. The mayor did not deny these facts but noted that the economic and fiscal conditions in Upsala were so bad that no increase could be given. The parties held four lengthy negotiation sessions, with neither party budging from its original position. A state mediator was called in and held four mediation sessions without budging either party from its position. The mediator withdrew from the case.

The union then proposed that the parties engage in fact-finding or arbitration, or both, in order to resolve the impasse. The mayor rejected the proposal, indicating that he was not required under state law to engage in either fact-finding or arbitration. No more formal sessions between the parties were held. Letters were exchanged, but neither side modified its original position. The contract expired June 30, 1991, with the town continuing to pay the wages and benefits prescribed in the expired agreement. The union members were angry but could not get the mayor to increase the town's proposal of a zero increase. September came and went, and there still was no resolution to the impasse.

Discussion Issues, Problems, and Questions

1. If you had been the mediator, would you have withdrawn after four sessions? Why or why not?
2. Should the mediator have tried to get back into the dispute after the parties continued to fail at a resolution? Do you think the mediator would have had more clout the second time around?
3. If the mediator felt that she was not making any headway in resolving the dispute, should she have urged the parties to accept fact-finding or arbitration?
4. What options, if any, does the union have in attempting to resolve the dispute?
5. If a similar set of circumstances occurred in the private sector, what do you think would have happened? Would the union have been in a stronger position? Why or why not?

Case 3: A Failure of Settlement: What is the Next Step?

The police officers of the town of Kappa are organized, and the union is one of five bargaining units with which the town has collective bargaining relations. For many years, negotiations with the police union came before those with the other bargaining units, and the settlement pattern for all unions was set by the police settlement. The police union of thirty officers was proud of its lead role in the town's negotiations with its unions. For many years, contract terms were worked out in two or three negotiation sessions, and the sessions were generally amicable as a result of the good working relationship between the town manager and the union leadership.

In the fall of 1989, the town manager retired, and a relatively young and inexperienced person was hired as manager. At about the same time, the union president and secretary-treasurer retired, and younger officers were elected to these positions. The new leadership of the town and the union had little time to get acquainted when the parties began negotiations in April 1990 for a new contract to replace the one expiring on June 30, 1990.

The police union proposed changes in wages, holidays, vacations, educational incentives, and outside detail rates. The new town manager proposed no changes in the contract, arguing that the town was facing fiscal constraints. The first bargaining session was more than a polite exchange of formal proposals; each side angrily and loudly attacked the position of the other. The following day, the local newspaper carried a complete story of the sessions, quoting the angry statements of both sides and the complete proposals of the parties. Each side then held a press conference, charging the other side with the leak to the press and with attempts to undermine the bargaining process.

At the second bargaining session, neither side was willing to make the first move of modifying its original position. The press was excluded from the session, but everyone seemed to feel that whatever happened at the session would be leaked to the press. The following day, the press did have the whole story. For the first time, the parties called on a state mediator to help in their negotiations. The mediator immediately imposed a gag order on the parties that worked reasonably well. Nevertheless, the mediator made no progress in getting the parties to modify their original positions.

After three sessions with the mediator, the parties agreed to go to fact-finding. The fact finder conducted a formal hearing at which each side had the opportunity to present facts and argue the merits of its position on each issue in dispute. The union defended its position on each issue by presenting supporting data from comparable communities in the area. The town presented data on its fiscal condition and contended that whatever was given to the police would set a pattern for all the other bargaining units.

On June 15, the fact-finder issued his findings and recommendations: reducing the union's proposed 5 percent wage increase to 3 percent, rejecting the holiday and vacation proposals of the union, which presumably would have been available to all the other bargaining units, and halving the union-proposed increases for educational incentives and detail rates, which would be applicable only to the firefighters' bargaining unit. The parties held another negotiation session to discuss the fact finder's recommendations. Both sides rejected the recommendations, and no progress toward a settlement was made.

Under state law, strikes by public employees were illegal, and arbitration of labor contract disputes was not mandatory. In an exchange of letters, the police union offered to go to arbitration on the issues in dispute. When the town rejected the offer, the union was faced with the dilemma of what to do next. The collective bargaining agreement expired on June 30, and by September 1, it was clear that the police union was losing by the failure to reach an agreement. The other public sector unions got tired of waiting for the local settlement of the police union and began their own negotiations with the town.

Without the right to strike, the police officers held informal discussions to determine how best to combat the town. One possibility was a slowdown or near stoppage of issuing parking violation tickets and traffic violation tickets. This tactic could strain the town's revenue and would put pressure on the town manager. Another possibility was the blue flu, with large numbers of officers calling in sick. This option would leave various duties uncovered or covered at a replacement cost of time and one-half.

Discussion Issues, Problems, and Questions

1. Considering that fact-finding involves recommendations that are not binding on the parties, why is this process successful in resolving disputes in many situations? What are the principal reasons for its failure?

2. If you were writing a state labor relations statute for public employees, would you include compulsory binding arbitration as the final step in the process, after the fact-finding? If arbitration were the final step in the process, would you be condemning fact-finding to failure? If arbitration were not included in the process, would you legalize the strike for public employees? Would you differentiate between public safety employees (police and fire) and other public employees in reference in the right to strike?

3. If you were the town manager of Kappa, how would you handle the situation if police officers engaged in the blue flu or failed to issue any parking violation tickets? Would you recognize such tactics if they were done slowly and with subtlety? Is it possible to write rules or statutes that would prevent such tactics?

Case 4: Politics and the Failure to Fund an Arbitration Award

Gamma is a medium-sized city on the East Coast, in a state with a collective bargaining statute that prohibits strikes in the public sector but permits arbitration that is binding on the executive office of the community but not on the legislative body. This means that the legislative body must act on any part of an arbitration award that requires funding, but it need not approve the expenditure of the funds.

In many previous collective bargaining negotiations between the city and its firefighters' union, the parties resolved their differences amicably. The wages and other benefits of the firefighters were always kept in the median group of comparable communities in the area, and both parties apparently accepted this structure.

In 1988 the mayor, who had held office for eighteen years, decided not to run for reelection, and two newcomers to politics engaged in a vicious and personal campaign. The firefighters' union had always been active in elections, and it supported candidate B against candidate A, actively campaigning in B's behalf, and becoming embroiled in the mudslinging campaign. None of the other public sector unions was actively involved in the election. Candidate A won by a slight margin, and his supporters won a majority of seats on the city council.

In early spring 1989, the firefighters' union and the city met in its first bargaining session over terms of a new labor contract, to be effective July 1, 1989. Much to the surprise of the union bargaining committee, the new mayor came to the bargaining session as a participant—the first time ever that a mayor had attended a session. Although an attorney was the city's spokesman, it was clear from the start that every proposal, counterproposal, and comment was being cleared by the mayor. It was also clear from some of the mayor's comments that he had not forgotten or forgiven that this union had supported his opponent in the election.

After three rather lengthy negotiation sessions, the parties realized they needed assistance. A state mediator was called in, and after three mediation sessions the mediator withdrew for lack of movement by either side. In the meantime, the city had started negotiations with the other bargaining units, and each settled quickly for a wage increase of from 4 to 6 percent, with a total package settlement calculated at 7 percent. In the firefighters' case, the union invoked fact-finding and on June 15, a fact-finding hearing was held. Posthearing briefs were filed, and the fact finder submitted her report and recommendations on July 17, 1989. She recommended a 5 percent wage increase effective July 1, 1989, and increases in fringe benefits amounting to an additional 2 percent. The union accepted the recommendations; the city did not. The parties then held a negotiation session, but still no progress was made in resolving the dispute. At this point, the local newspapers published the fact finder's recommendations and the reaction of the parties to the them. The case was then moved to arbitration.

Because of summer vacations and the normal problems of finding an appropriate date for the parties and the arbitrator, the first hearing date was in mid-September, and a second arbitration hearing session was held on October 2. Posthearing briefs were filed on October 30, and the arbitrator handed down his award on November 20. With some very minor variations, the arbitrator accepted the fact finder's recommendations as his arbitration award. The newspapers again picked up the story and repeated the mayor's opposition to the fact-finder's recommendations.

Abiding by state law, the mayor presented the arbitrator's award to the city council, indicated his support, and asked the council to fund the monetary aspects of the award. The motion to fund the award was defeated by a majority of one vote. The only option open to the union was to meet with the city and try to negotiate a different agreement.

Discussion Issues, Problems, and Questions

1. What arguments can you make to defend a process in which the legislative body of a city or town can refuse to fund an arbitration award?

2. Since the executive officer of the city had approved proceeding into arbitration, should the legislative body have the right to reject the arbitrator's award? Should the union membership have an equal right to reject an award if it is dissatisfied with the results?

3. Do you think the mayor really supported the arbitration award, or was he going through the legal motions required by state law? If he was in favor of funding the award, do you think he could have convinced a majority of the council to vote in favor of funding it?
4. Where does this process leave the union? If you were the union president, what would you do? What would you propose to the union membership?

Case 5. A Unique Procedure for Resolving Labor Disputes

The town of Brookstone is a small bedroom community about fifty miles from Boston with a town manager form of government. It has a police force of eight officers, all of whom are members of the Brookstone Police Union. The union was certified as the bargaining agent in 1988, and with the assistance of a Boston attorney, the union and town reached a collective bargaining agreement after four bargaining sessions. The contract ran from July 1, 1988 through June 30, 1990.

In March 1990, the parties began negotiations for a successor agreement. After four sessions, the parties filed a petition with the Massachusetts Joint Labor-Management Committee for Municipal Police and Fire, asking it to take jurisdiction over the matter. A JLMC staff investigator assigned to the case visited the parties and reported his findings to the JLMC. Jurisdiction was taken, and the staff investigator held several mediation sessions with the parties. The parties remained far apart on wages, clothing allowance, educational allowance, and detail rates.

The staff investigator briefed the senior staff representative for labor and for management, and they joined him in the next mediation session. The senior staff representative for labor met with the union bargaining committee, while the senior staff representative for management met with the town's bargaining committee. In these private sessions, the respective bargaining committees were informed of JLMC policies and procedures, and the patterns of settlements that might have some impact on the current negotiations. The parties moved a bit closer on the detail rate and the clothing allowance but reached no agreement.

A police union committee member and a management committee member who happened to be a town manager were assigned to the case. They attended the next negotiation session, and because of their own experiences as a union leader and a town manager, they made considerable progress toward a resolution of the issues. After the session, the two JLMC members conferred with each other and discovered that each side was willing to make further concessions but could not do so openly for political reasons. The committee representatives held another meeting with the parties and convinced them to present their positions on the open issues to a tripartite committee of the JLMC.

On July 15, a tripartite panel of the JLMC was convened, consisting of the chair of the JLMC and the labor and management committee members who had visited the parties previously. The parties presented their respective positions on the open issues and also their arguments to support the positions. After the hearing, the panel met and discussed each of the issues, seeking a fair and equitable resolution of all the items in dispute.

Discussion Issues, Problems, and Questions

1. What aspects of the procedures of the JLMC do you consider relatively unique? What would you recommend of these procedures for all other public sector unions?
2. Why were the union and town bargaining committees more willing to talk to members of the JLMC than to staff personnel of the committee?
3. The police bargaining unit had eight police officers. Should the JLMC have spent so much staff and committee member time on such a small local union? If the parties had been charged for all services given them by the JLMC, do you think the parties could have afforded them?

Appendix: Rules of the Massachusetts Joint Labor-Management Committee for Municipal Police and Fire, Adopted May 6, 1988

The purpose of the Joint Labor-Management Committee is to encourage the parties to collective bargaining disputes involving municipal police officers and firefighters to agree on the terms of collective bargaining agreements or the procedures to resolve particular disputes. The Committee shall make every effort to encourage the parties to engage in good faith negotiations to reach settlement and a constructive long-term relationship.

The Operations of the Committee

1. Each part of the Committee, professional police officers, professional firefighters and representatives of the cities and towns shall designate a chairman of its group within the Committee to facilitate consultation and communications. Each part of the Committee shall establish procedures by which it shall designate a chairman and the terms of office.
2. In matters exclusively pertaining to municipal firefighters, committee members nominated for appointment by professional police officer organizations shall not vote, and in matters exclusively pertaining to municipal police officers, committee members nominated for appointment by professional firefighter organizations shall not vote.
3. All Committee members shall be eligible to vote on matters of common and general interest.
4. The number of votes of Committee members representing the local government advisory committee and the number of votes of Committee members representing the professional firefighter or police organizations entitled to vote on any matter coming before the Committee shall be equal.
5. The Chairman may cast the deciding vote on any matter relating to a dispute concerning negotiations over the terms and provisions of a collective bargaining agreement, including any decision to exercise jurisdiction over a dispute. The Chairman shall be the chief administrative officer of the Committee. The Vice-Chairman shall assist the Chairman and may be authorized by the Chairman to act for him in his absence and shall have the full powers of the Chairman when so authorized and he shall vote only in the absence of the Chairman.
6. The Committee shall comply with the Open Meeting Law of the Commonwealth as amended. That statute, Chapter 30, Section 11A½ (3) provides that executive sessions may be held "to

discuss strategy with respect to collective bargaining . . . and to conduct collective bargaining sessions," including related mediation and such sessions may be closed by the Committee.

7. A quorum shall consist of one member of the Committee representing the local government advisory committee and one member of the Committee representing the professional firefighter organizations and one member of the Committee representing the professional police officers organizations and the Chairman or Vice-Chairman.

8. The Committee expects that its members shall regularly attend meetings of the Committee. However, professional police organizations, professional fire organizations, and the local government advisory committee shall specify alternate members to represent their respective members, subject to the approval of the full Committee, for a term of one year (subject to reappointment) to assure that the work of the Committee may go forward. Alternative members are expected regularly to attend meetings of the Committee.

9. The Committee shall appoint one full-time senior staff person nominated by the members of the Committee representing the local government advisory committee and one full-time senior staff person nominated by the members of the Committee representing the professional police officer and professional firefighter organizations. The two senior staff persons shall work together to further the purpose of the Committee. They may be assigned by the Committee through the Chairman to gather facts, to facilitate negotiations, to mediate, and otherwise to encourage agreement between parties.

10. The Committee may specify other staff positions in accordance with law and within the budget. The Chairman shall supervise such staff. The Committee may also appoint special mediators, fact finders or neutrals to facilitate the resolution of particular cases.

II. The Involvement of the Committee in Disputes

1. The Committee shall have oversight responsibility for all collective bargaining negotiations involving municipal police officers and firefighters.

2. The Committee shall request the executive Office of Labor, the Board of Conciliation and Arbitration and the Labor Relations Commission each to designate a person with whom the Committee shall consult these Agencies on particular cases to assure co-operative relations and consistent activities in the interest of improved collective bargaining and dispute resolution.

3. Should either party or the parties acting jointly to a municipal police and fire collective bargaining negotiations believe a dispute is unresolved and warrants mediation, the party or both parties shall petition the Committee for the exercise of jurisdiction. Such petitions shall identify the issues in dispute, the parties and the efforts of the parties to resolve the dispute.

(a) The Committee shall forthwith review the petition and shall make a determination within thirty (30) days of the receipt of the petition whether to exercise jurisdiction over the dispute. If the Committee declines to exercise jurisdiction over the dispute or fails to act within thirty (30) days of receipt of the petition of jurisdiction, the petition shall automatically be referred to the Board of Conciliation and Arbitration for disposition in accordance with its procedures.

(b) The Committee may subsequently at any stage after consultation with the Board of Conciliation and Arbitration remove the dispute from the jurisdiction of the Board and handle the case as if it had retained jurisdiction at the outset. The Committee may, at any time, remand to the Board any dispute in which the Committee has exercised jurisdiction. The Committee's decisions on jurisdiction are to be formally communicated to the Board of Conciliation and Arbitration and to the parties.

4. After a petition has been filed with the Committee, the parties to any municipal police and firefighter negotiations shall furnish the assigned field investigator the following information:

(a) Copies of request to bargain and proposals of each side.

(b) Notification of all pending unfair labor practice proceedings between the parties.

(c) Collective bargaining agreements and relevant personnel ordinances, bylaws, and rules and regulations including wage and salary and benefit schedules.

(d) Such other information as the field investigator may reasonably require for the Committee.

5. The Committee may, at its discretion, and on its own initiative, exercise jurisdiction in any dispute over the negotiations of the terms of a collective bargaining agreement involving municipal firefighters or police officers. The Committee may also exercise jurisdiction in any dispute concerning job titles over which the parties have negotiated or in any dispute over proposals to remove specific job titles from collective bargaining for individuals and performing certain specified management duties.

6. The Committee or its representatives, field investigators or staff mediators may meet with the parties to a dispute, conduct formal or informal conferences, and take other steps including mediation to encourage the parties to agree on terms of a collective bargaining agreement or the procedures to resolve the dispute. The Committee shall make every effort to encourage the parties to engage in good faith bargaining to reach settlement through negotiations or mediation.

7. In certain disputes that persist, the Committee may order factfinding and appoint a factfinder outside the Committee to report the facts, mediate the dispute and make recommendations for resolution of the disputed issues. The Committee may on occasion designate its members, including the Chairman or Vice Chairman, to perform such functions. The Committee shall determine the procedures for the distribution and any release of the report.

8. In dispute resolution conducted by other than the Committee or its members or staff, the parties shall share and pay equally the costs involved in such resolution, provided, however, that pursuant to a vote of the Committee and subject to the availability of funds for the purpose thereof, said costs may be paid by the Committee.

9. The Committee shall have the power to administer oaths and to require by subpoena the attendance and testimony of witnesses, the production of books, records, and other evidence relative to or pertinent to the issues in the dispute.

10 In any dispute before the Committee in which it concludes that a study of the financial ability of the municipality to meet costs may facilitate the resolution of the dispute, it may request the Commissioner of Revenue to make such a study specifying various factors to be taken into consideration.

11. When the parties to a municipal police or fire collective bargaining negotiation jointly design their own dispute resolution procedures, they may divest the Committee of jurisdiction by presenting a written agreement of their procedures to the Committee; provided, however, that the Committee finds that said procedures provide for a final resolution of the dispute, without resort to strike, job action, or lockout; and provided, further that if the Committee subsequently finds that either of the parties fails to abide by said procedures, the Committee shall assume jurisdiction of the dispute.

III. Procedures in Disputes That Have Remained Unsolved for an Unreasonable Period of Time Resulting in the Apparent Exhaustion of the Processes of Collective Bargaining.

(Section 3 (a) of Chapter 589 of the Acts of 1987.)

1. In a dispute, over which the Committee has taken jurisdiction, and which the Committee determines issues in dispute have remained unsolved for an unreasonable period of time resulting in the apparent exhaustion of the processes of collective bargaining, the Committee shall hold a hearing to identify:
(a)   The issues remaining in dispute;
(b)   The current position of the parties;
(c)   The view of the parties as to how the continuing dispute should be resolved;
(d)   The preferences of the parties as to the mechanism to be followed in order to reach a final agreement between the parties; and
(e)   Other relevant questions.

2. If the Committee thereafter finds there is an apparent exhaustion of the processes of collective bargaining which constitutes a potential threat to public welfare, it shall so notify the parties of its findings. Within ten days of such notification, the Committee shall also notify the parties of its intent to invoke such procedures and mechanisms as it deems appropriate, and it has been authorized by legislation to use, for the resolution of the collective bargaining negotiations.

3. In any dispute involving the financial ability of the municipality to meet costs, the assistance of a report of the Commissioner of

Revenue is to be requested, if a current report had not been secured earlier in dispute resolution efforts of the Committee. (See II-10 above).

4. Any decision or determination resulting from the above procedures determined by the Committee, if supported by material and substantive evidence on the whole record, shall be subject to the approval by the legislative body of a funding request as set forth in the statute, binding upon the public employer and employee organization, as set forth in chapter one hundred fifty E of the General Laws, and may be enforced at the instance of either party or the Committee in superior court in equity.

IV. Other Procedural Matters

1. The Committee may assemble a file of collective bargaining agreements and wage, and salary and fringe benefit data and other statistical information to facilitate constructive collective bargaining and dispute resolution.

2. The Committee shall review periodically the operations of these Rules in light of experience and in view of suggestions received from interested parties and appropriate legislative committees.

3. The Committee shall prepare an annual fiscal year report of its activities to submit to the Governor and to the Legislature.

4. These proposed Procedural Rules shall be filed with the clerks of the Senate and House of Representatives of the Commonwealth of Massachusetts. In accordance with the procedures specified in the statute, the Committee shall subsequently adopt final regulations which shall supersede the Rules of July, 1979.

7

Public Intervention in Public Sector Bargaining

A number of unions that had early success in organizing private sector enterprises made efforts, most of them unsuccessful, to organize workers in the public sector in such places as naval shipyards, the Government Printing Office, and arsenals. These efforts were hindered by a number of factors: the strike ban in the public sector, the sovereign services performed by government employees responsible for continuity and for providing emergency services, and the resistance of taxpayers to following the free market and raising taxes to pay. In addition, public employees were generally viewed as having better job security and better economic benefits than workers in the private sector.

The system of labor relations in the public sector is influenced by a complex network of forces that include public policy, social and economic forces, political realities, the past, and special characteristics of work and organization in public bureaucracies.[1] Although there are many indications that public sector collective bargaining has been gradually assuming more of the characteristics of collective bargaining in the private sector, there still remain many differences. One of the key differences is that public sector unions are faced with the issue of distribution of political power among those groups pressing claims on the government.[2] Case 1 of this chapter concerns this issue. According to a review of public sector unionism, Richard B. Freeman finds:

A fundamental difference between public and private sector collective bargaining is that public sector unions, more so than private sector unions, can influence the employer behavior through the political process. The principal reason for this is that public sector employees help elect both the executive and legislative branches of government and thus play a role in determining the agenda for those facing them at the bargaining table. . . .

. . . Although it is true that public employers do not face competition in their locality, they are subject to the discipline of a budget and, in the long run, to exit and entry of residents and businesses.[3]

Freeman holds that because of the political nature of public sector collective bargaining, union goals are more likely to include the size of budgets and of employment than do the goals of private sector unions.[4] Case 2 addresses this matter.

In public sector bargaining, power on the employer's side is shared by administrators, elected officials, and legislative bodies, and what often begins as a variant of private sector bargaining ends up by becoming an extension of politics. Thus, public sector bargaining is frequently a multilateral process, with more than two distinct parties involved in such a way that a clear dichotomy between the employee and management organizations does not always exist.[5]

The Public Interest

There is little doubt that the general public usually takes a much greater and personal interest in public sector union activities and collective bargaining than in private sector union activities. Local and national services—garbage collection, postal services, schools, and municipal hospitals—affect the public directly.

The public is the consumer of the services of the public sector; it pays and has no choice of market. The general public sees a direct tie between the compensation and other benefits public employees receive and the costs to taxpayers. At the local levels of government, public employees are also voting members of the community and neighbors of the private sector employees. How this mix exists in any community (town, city, or state) may determine the leverage and power any single public sector union may have. Case 3 shows the effectiveness of public opposition. If all public employees living in a community are organized and the various unions cooperate actively in the political process or in the collective bargaining process, labor has considerable strength. In the fourth case this issue is critical in the settlement. In many communities across the nation, the political roles of teacher, police, and firefighter unions show this strength. In many instances, public sector unions sponsor candidates to public positions—mayor, school committee, select-man, city council—and in these positions the incumbents partici-pate on the employer side in the collective bargaining process. If, however, the various public sector unions compete with each other, their collective strength is dissipated, and management gains more relative power. On the other hand, if administrators and legislators do not work cooperatively, this may weaken the management posi-tion in the collective bargaining process.

Superimposed on this public sector labor relations picture are the constant and growing problems of municipal budgets that are inadequate to meet the political and public interest claims made on them. This problem is particularly troublesome in a declining econ-omy, with taxpayers losing jobs and tax revenues falling. Munici-palities constantly face conflicting demands from various groups for services and funds, and frequently new money must be found to satisfy vocal and politically powerful groups. In many cases tax-payers balk at higher taxes, yet they continue to seek better school programs, improved school facilities, cleaner streets, more police protection, improved care for the homeless, and a better communi-ty hospital. Such demands have always been placed before the administrators of all communities, and how they were met or not met depended on a complex of economic, political, and social fac-tors in the community. And especially since the mid-1970s, increas-ing pressures on city and state officials to reduce government expenditures have combined with a growing public sentiment for "financial responsibility" in government.[6] In 1992, for example, negotiations of a number of public sector bargaining units were set-tled for a zero wage increase as a trade for no layoffs.

In the public sector, cities and towns engaged in collective bar-gaining may have four or more bargaining units, each competing with the others for scarce funds. A typical community may have collective bargaining contracts with police officers, firefighters, teachers, general public service employees, and maintenance employees; some communities also have separate bargaining units with school custodians, school maintenance workers, and clerical workers. It is not unlikely that each union endeavors to negotiate a contract with benefits that exceed those of the other bargaining units. A common position by a public employer is to offer the same wage and benefit package to all of the bargaining units. Howard Block has noted:

> In many, if not most, inability-to-pay situations, the impasse is not due to the economic cost of reaching an agreement with the employee group directly involved in the negotiations. . . . The underlying problem for management is to avoid a settlement figure with one group which arouses unrealistic expectancies among large numbers or other employees who are being pressed to go along with a uniform wage policy pegged at a lower rate.[7]

From the public union's perspective, it may be faced with a multifaceted opponent: appointed managers, elected mayors, elected finance committees, and elected city councils. In which person or groups the power lies varies from community to community and over time. Further, even a person or group in the management structure that appears to have relatively little direct power to shape a collective bargaining settlement may have the negative power to block one. This situation is surely different from the one normally found in the private sector.

Both parties to a public sector collective bargaining arrangement face possible intervention by public groups that may not be direct participants in the labor negotiations. On management's side, the groups that may intervene include those who are selected or elected as public officials; on the labor side, the participants (the union members) are members of the general public who participate in the election and selection of the public officials. In addition, various general public groups (businesses, parent-teacher associations, civic groups, taxpayers, taxpayer associations, and property owners) may pressure and lobby public officials in regard to ongoing labor negotiations or to a tentative settlement reached by the parties. Unions that are nonparticipants to the bargaining process may also lobby and apply pressure on the participants.

In various situations, the general public or segments of the public intervene in public sector bargaining. A relatively common situation of public intervention occurs when the last of a number of bargaining units attempts to break a uniform settlement that all other units had agreed to. Once such information becomes public knowledge, business and taxpayer groups may start pressuring elected public officials to reject the demand. The other bargaining units may also intervene by calling on public officials, who depend on their support and vote, to reject the demand. On the other hand, these other bargaining units may have a "me too" clause in their agreements that provides for wage increases to match the wage adjustments of other settlements in the community. Whether such intervention by other unions occurs openly or covertly depends on the relations among the various labor unions and their officers.

Public intervention may occur when unions agree to help secure funding for a settlement. For example, the public official in charge of negotiations announces to all the public sector unions that because of the town's financial situation, it is offering a zero increase in the first year of a two-year contract and a 2 percent increase in the second year. Here, the various unions are likely to join together to lobby elected officials to find public funds to finance a wage increase in the first year of the contract by curtailing other services. Pressure by union members, their families, and friends may be sufficient to change the offer. Other groups may also lobby the public officials in an effort not to raise taxes and not to change the zero offer. Public officials will undoubtedly be under conflicting pressure by various groups in the community.

A third possible situation involves a public sector union that must negotiate with a public official whose election the union had openly opposed. If the official is vindictive and offers the union a smaller wage package than was offered to all other public sector unions, the union could try to sidestep the official and lobby the legislative body for support, although in most political jurisdictions the legislative body may have no authority over collective bargaining and contract settlements. Or it could lobby the public official's political supporters for assistance, but this may or may not work. The case is reasonably clear that politics has intervened in the collective bargaining process, with no readily attainable solution.

Indeed, there are relatively few situations in public sector bargaining in which general public intervention, direct or indirect, does not occur. A management representative in the bargaining process represents the public at large and is selected or elected for that purpose; however, he or she may also be elected by trade union support and be responsive to a trade union constituency that makes end runs to the legislature. By participating in the negotiations, the representative is involved in public intervention in the bargaining process. Additionally, union members, whose representatives sit on one side of the bargaining table, are voters in the general public who elect the public officials who sit on the opposite side of the bargaining table.

From a slightly different perspective, one can readily see the general interest in the operations and functions of public service employees such as police, firefighters, teachers, librarians, and trash collectors. Unions can galvanize pressure on the employer by arguing safety, or minimum staffing, or class size in the public schools. The public concern for safety on the streets may affect the police union's bargaining on the number of officers required for each police cruiser, the number of cruisers compared to officers walking the beat, and the number of hours per day or per week an officer is permitted to work outside details. The right of police officers to select their working shifts on the basis of seniority may also be an issue of public concern. Would there be a sufficient number of younger officers on the most desirable shifts? In many cities police union contracts require financial compensation at premium rates for off-duty court appearances, and it has been alleged that officers, especially those on evening or night duty, may see a financial incentive to make arrests that necessitate a court appearance the next day.[8] Clearly there would be public concern about such a practice if it appeared to exist in any community. Another issue that has resulted in public concern and public intervention is one involving residency—whether a police officer need reside in the city of employment. Cities argue that residing implies a commitment to the city and to its improvement and that the officers should be readily available for call-in, callback, and standby. Unions argue that police officers should be free to live in the suburbs, where the streets are safe and the schools sound.[9] Additionally, police and firefighters may not be able to afford to live in wealthy towns.

General public concern and possible intervention in the matter of firefighters' unions also involve residency requirements and seniority as the basis for shift bidding. Here too the public is concerned about public safety and may view these matters as important. The staffing issue—how many firefighters per shift and how many per piece of equipment—is pertinent here.

Where unions have raised these staffing issues, generally as a safety issue for the firefighters but also for a better response to a fire, the additional costs become a public issue. Inevitably, the argument is made that firefighters spend too much time sitting around in the fire station. Nevertheless, there is likely to be a segment of the general public that will support the union's demand for additional staffing on the grounds of greater security and protection. Other sectors of the general public may hold that the cost of additional staffing outweighs the possible benefits. How strongly each of these groups feels about the relative merits of the union's demand may influence the amount and intensity of intervention.

In some states, the scope of collective bargaining, especially as it pertains to arbitration, is specified and limited by statute.[10] These statutes thus involve a clear case of public intervention in the collective bargaining process.

Public intervention is also indicated by a 1987 Massachusetts statute involving arbitration awards for police and firefighters.[11] These awards were made binding on the executive of the city or town but not on the legislative body in cases involving the appropriation of funds. If the legislative body does not approve appropriations for the award, the matter is returned to the parties for further bargaining. In other words, the legislative body has veto power over the financial terms of an arbitration award, allowing politics to intervene in the collective bargaining process.

In many communities, the school department budget is a significant part of the total budget, and public intervention in the collective bargaining with the teachers' union is not uncommon, because of the costs and apparent benefits. A common issue in collective bargaining is class size, and groups that have children in the school system may view small classes as an educational advantage. Another possible issue in teachers' union negotiations is the amount of time teachers spend in the classroom. Here the sector of the public favoring small class size may oppose the union's demand to reduce the teachers' time in the classroom. The issue of lunchroom and recess duties may come up in bargaining. If teachers are not involved in such duties, nonteachers must be employed to perform them. Here the costs are clear but any benefits to the general public uncertain. Generally property owners with no children in the school system oppose and may actively intervene in any teachers' union proposal that may add costs and possibly raise taxes.

Public Participation

Whereas public intervention in the public sector bargaining process is clear and frequently obvious, public participation in the process may not always be open and obvious. For that matter, those who represent the municipality in negotiations with a public sector union may vary, depending on the issue or the administrative structure of the community. A union may find itself negotiating with a mayor, the finance committee of a city council, the city manager, the civil service commission, the city personnel director, the manager of a department, the budget director, the city attorney, or any outside attorney. Every one of these represents the public in some fashion. Who is the final authority may vary with the issue and the case. For administrative issues, it is likely to be the executive or administrative branch; for financial issues, it is likely to be the legislature.

The structure of collective bargaining in any unit of the public sector is generally set by the statutory authority of the scope of bargaining. Where pensions, health insurance, sick leave, and other benefits are set for all state employees by statute, collective bargaining is limited to the scope authorized by the legislature. The administrative or executive branch of the political unit is generally authorized by statute to negotiate with the public sector unions. State courts have limited the scope of bargaining based on interpretation of state legislation, forbidding negotiations on certain issues and ceding other issues to a civil service commission. Specific issues within the authority of the administrative or executive branch are sometimes ceded to experts, such as the fire chief on staffing or the superintendent of schools on class size. Compensation and wages are normally limited by the money provided by the appropriate legislative body, but money items can be postponed, juggled, or traded off for other issues to balance dollars and administrative responsibilities.

Political forces and pressure groups may also shape the allocation of responsibility for collective bargaining. A strong mayor or governor may shape collective bargaining as a result of their office or because they are politically powerful persons. One possible consequence of the fragmentation in management bargaining responsibility is the use by public sector unions of the end run, which may be considered participation or intervention. Public employee organizations generally have friends and supporters among elected officials; at every level of government, unions and public employee associations devote considerable amounts of resources in support of the election of particular candidates.[12] Regardless of who has the real authority, many different players participate in the bargaining process.

There is no standard procedure or process for general public participation in public sector collective bargaining. In many situations, the effect is the same whether the general public intervenes or participates in the collective bargaining process. What is clear is that groups of the general public may have a significant impact on the results of collective bargaining through intervention or participation in the process, depending on such factors as the size of the group, the tactics used, and the political power of the groups. Public intervention may attract media attention, but it is more likely to occur behind the scenes, without publicity.

In the public sector, the question has been debated as to whether union security provisions should be permitted by negotiation or prohibited by statute. In view of the history of these provisions in private sector bargaining, one can readily conclude that mandating such provisions by statute clearly represents public participation in the collective bargaining process. Similarly, when a state, by statute, excludes from the collective bargaining process a specific subject or issue, this too is public participation. For example, a state statute may specifically provide that no municipal employer is required to negotiate over subjects of minimum staffing of shift coverage with an employee organization representing police officers and firefighters, presumably because the public interest outweighs the interests of the police and the firefighters. Such a mandate is a clear case of public participation in the collective bargaining process.

The concept of comparable worth has involved considerable public participation in the bargaining process. Some unions and other groups have lobbied outside the normal avenues of collective bargaining for this concept. By 1989, six states had increased the pay of public employees in traditionally female occupations, and several other states had begun to reexamine their pay structures and policies.[13] Thus, despite collective bargaining agreements, state statutes have changed (increased) the wage levels of specific occupations and thereby changed what might have been traditional wage relationships between occupations and between collective bargaining agreements. It is likely that additional states will increase the pay of public employees in traditionally female occupations. Although the concept of comparable worth is equally applicable to both the public and the private sectors, its supporters have lobbied mainly in the public sector, and especially at the state level. On the whole, state bargaining agreements cover a wider and more diverse range of job classifications than in the private sector.

The issue of subcontracting certain aspects of an operation or service has been of concern to unions in both the public and private sectors because of the effects of subcontracting on the prospects of layoffs and overall job insecurity. Although subcontracting on an ad hoc basis has been going on for many decades in the private sector, there has been a recent surge of subcontracting and privatization in the public sector. Some public services are easily transferred to a private contractor, and in most such situations, the public employee has little or no recourse. Subcontracting brings into conflict two fundamental rights and interests. Employers view the issue as their right to manage the enterprise, to determine what services should be rendered to the public, and to decide how these services can be delivered most effectively and efficiently. Employees and their unions see the issue as their right to share in the determination of the terms and conditions of employment.[14] Increased financial strain in the public sector will provide greater pressure on governments to engage in subcontracting or in other practices that will reduce the size of the public work force. Thus, various sectors of the public may participate in the bargaining process in an effort to reduce the payroll costs of the government.

Conclusions

There is often a thin line between intervention and participation in a public sector collective bargaining relationship, and various individuals and groups that are not direct participants in a collective bargaining relationship intervene and participate in that process. The general public has a vested interest in the results of public sector collective bargaining, as do various individuals and special interest groups. Unions are also part of a special group, and they too intervene and participate in the collective bargaining process. In a democratic society, it is inevitable that the general public and special interest groups will be interested in the results of collective bargaining in the public sector and will intervene and participate whenever possible.

Questions for Discussion

1. There is little doubt that various sectors of the general public feel they have a legitimate right to intervene or participate in the bargaining process involving public sector employees. Inasmuch as these sectors have little right or opportunity to intervene or participate in bargaining in the private sector, why should they participate in the public sector process? Are there any basic differences between public and private sector employees? If you identify basic differences, are they sufficiently large as to call for different treatments?

2. If you were a mayor of a large industrial city, how would you feel about a group of the general public intervening in your negotiations with the firefighters' union by publicly criticizing your position? If you could effectively block the group from intervening, would you do so? Why or why not? Would you feel any differently if the group wanted to participate in the negotiations process?

3. If you were a member of a city council that had the final responsibility of funding the financial changes in a collective bargaining agreement, would you want to intervene or otherwise participate in the collective bargaining process for which the mayor has the prime responsibility? Why or why not? If you did not intervene or participate in the process, would you feel free to vote down a settlement that the mayor negotiated with the union? What would you consider legitimate reasons for this action?

4. From the perspective of the employer who has the legal

responsibility to negotiate with the public sector union, is there any significant difference between intervention and participation? From the perspective of the public sector union, is there any significant difference? Do you believe that a difference should be made, giving greater legitimacy to one than to the other?

5. If you were a large employer in a community and negotiated regularly with the International Association of Machinists, how would you react if an environmentalist group tried to intervene in your negotiations with the union? If, at the same time, it was leaked by the press that the mayor was considering a 7 percent wage increase in his negotiations with a number of public sector unions, would you try to intervene? Would it make it easier for you to intervene if your discussions with your union were for a wage increase of approximately 5 percent while the union was demanding 8 percent? Would it make it easier for you to intervene if you felt a 7 percent increase to public sector workers would raise your property tax significantly?

Case 1: Union Political Action Affects a Settlement

The mid-sized town of Middlebury has had good labor relations with its police and firefighter unions for a number of years. The mayor and the town council developed a friendly relationship with the officers of the unions, and many of the union members know a number of the town officials on a personal basis. After sixteen years in office, the mayor decided not to run for reelection in 1989; in the previous three elections, he had run unopposed. Four of the five members of the town council also decided not to run for reelection in 1989.

As soon as the mayor announced he was not up for reelection, two local businessmen announced their candidacies. Both sought the support of various groups in the town, and for unknown reasons, the police union came out in favor of candidate A and the firefighters' union in favor of candidate B. Ten candidates were vying for the five seats on the town council, and none was directly tied to either of the two mayoral candidates. Neither of the two unions officially supported any of the candidates for the council, although a number of union members and their families did campaign for some of the candidates for the council.

Candidate A defeated candidate B by a narrow margin. The one town council incumbent was reelected, and four new members joined the council. Three months after the election, the mayor began negotiations with the police and the firefighters' unions for successor agreements to the ones expiring on June 30, 1990. The negotiations with the police union, which had supported the mayor's election, went smoothly; after three sessions, the mayor and the union president issued a joint statement indicating a settlement for a 4 percent wage increase and some minor adjustments that were considered more or less costless. The negotiations with the firefighters' union, which had supported the mayor's opponent for election, did not go well. The union's initial demand was for a 6 percent wage increase, but after the police union settled for 4 percent, the firefighters lowered their demand to 4 percent. The mayor countered with a 3.5 percent increase and asked for some give-backs that were minor in nature but nevertheless irritated the union negotiating committee. It was clear to both sides from comments made at the bargaining sessions that the election aftermath was affecting the negotiations.

The parties held ten negotiating sessions without reaching an agreement. On July 1 the police officers received their wage adjustment under their new contract, while the firefighters continued working without a contract. In early October, after four more negotiation sessions, the union accepted the 3.5 percent wage offer when the mayor withdrew his demand for some give-backs. The agreement was signed and subsequently submitted to the town council for funding.

After considerable discussion about the dire financial picture of the town, a majority of the five-member council voted not to fund the increase provided for in the firefighters' agreement. In reporting this story, the town newspaper questioned whether the vote was a political reaction by three council members who had gotten no support in their election from the firefighters. It also noted that the town did not have a budget problem and questioned how large the deficit was.

There were no specified rules as to what was the next step to resolve the matter.

Discussion Issues, Problems, and Questions

1. Clearly the negotiation stance of the mayor and the rejection of the negotiated agreement by the council were formed more by political than by economic considerations. If you were the union president, what steps would you take to try to get the matter of a new contract resolved? Looking back at the situation prior to the election, what would you have advised the union with respect to political action?

2. How do you account for the intervention of the town council in the collective bargaining process of the police union? If the town council had a legitimate role to play in the process, should it have participated in the negotiation sessions along with the mayor? If you were the mayor, would you have invited the town council to participate with you in all the negotiation sessions with the firefighters' union, to ensure that a majority of the council supported the town's proposals and its tentative agreement?

3. If you were the mayor, would you consider the action of the council as an intervention in your role as employer? Would you attempt to convince the council to approve the negotiated agreement so as to bolster your political prestige?

4. If you were a voting citizen of the town, how would you react to this standoff? Who would you think took the more sound position: the mayor or the town council? How would you suggest resolving the immediate matter? What would you suggest be done in order to prevent this kind of problem from occurring in the future?

5. How would you rationalize, in nonpolitical terms, why the police union was given a 4 percent wage increase while the firefighters' union received a 3.5 percent increase?

Case 2: Public Interest and Union Wages

The city of Royal has had collective bargaining relations with six bargaining units for many years, and because of its prosperous situation, the city employees were considered to be about the highest paid among comparable communities in the region. Despite similar wage adjustment among the six bargaining units, there were significant differences in wage levels, and over time, the dollar differential widened because of the practice of granting percentage wage adjustments. The unions competed with each other in an effort to get more than the other unions, but the competition was generally friendly because the wage adjustments usually were generous.

In 1990 a severe recession hit the region, including Royal. Unemployment in the private sector rose sharply, and the city's revenue dropped precipitously. The mayor put a hiring freeze on all city departments. To fill any vacancy required special action by the city's personnel director and the mayor.

Early in spring 1991, the mayor began negotiations with the various unions. Serious negotiations started first with union A, the smallest of the six units and the one that had fallen furthest behind the others. The union protested its wage level as it compared historically to those of the other bargaining units and also noted that its wage levels had not been maintained relative to the wage levels of comparable communities in the area. The mayor seemed surprised that this bargaining unit had not kept up relative to the other city units and expressed doubt that Royal had not continued to be the leader among the comparable communities in wages. The mayor agreed to survey the comparable communities. At the next bargaining session, he conceded that the union was right; its wage levels were exceeded by those in three of the comparable communities. The union indicated that it recognized the city's financial problems and proposed a 2 percent increase, which would bring it just above the comparable communities.

The mayor was in a dilemma. He recognized the validity of the union's arguments and agreed that a 2 percent increase would be fair and equitable; however, he knew he could not finance a 2 percent increase for the other five bargaining units. The mayor was also aware that it would be politically unwise to grant a 2 percent wage increase to the organized city employees while serious wage cuts and layoffs were occurring in the private sector.

The discussions between the mayor and union A leaked to the other unions, which then individually requested a 2 percent wage adjustment. When the mayor indicated he would not give that increase, the five unions issued a joint press release, stating that the mayor was favoring union A over the other unions and that this would break the uniform pattern that had been practiced for almost twenty years. This was clearly direct intervention in the bargaining process of union A. Some general public groups joined the fray, demanding that the mayor treat all public employees equally.

Discussion Issues, Problems, and Questions

1. In view of the mayor's previous experience in negotiating with six different bargaining units of city employees, should he have expected this kind of a problem? What could be done at the outset to avoid the problem? Once the issue arose, is there anything the mayor could do to resolve the matter and satisfy all parties? If he cannot completely resolve the matter, what alternatives does he have to minimize the problem? What can he do to minimize his own political losses?

2. If you were president of union A, would you continue to push hard for the 2 percent wage adjustment, even at the risk of jeopardizing your long-term relationship with the other public sector unions? If you held fast to your position to gain the 2 percent what do you think would happen to the mayor's political career? If you thought it would jeopardize the mayor's political career, would you press for it nevertheless? How would your own career be affected by your demanding the 2 percent increase?

3. If you were the president of one of the other public service unions, what would your position be? Would you insist on intervening in the negotiations between the city and union A? How would you go about trying to get the 2 percent wage increase for your members too?

4. If you were the editor of the local newspaper, would you publish an editorial on the matter of the 2 percent wage increase for city employees? If you decided to do an editorial, who would you favor, and what would you recommend to resolve the dispute? Would you urge the general public to oppose any wage increase for the city employees?

5. Suppose you were the president of a relatively large private sector union in the city that had been forced to take a 2 percent wage cut in order to avoid a substantial layoff. How would you react to the situation of the mayor's agreeing to a 2 percent wage increase for only one of the public sector unions? Would you actively intervene in the negotiation process? Would you inter-

vene on your own, or would you join the other public sector unions in an effort to keep wages down? From the point of view of the politics in your own union, how do you think your members would react to your protesting a wage increase?

Case 3: Public Opposition to a Settlement

Granfield has had reasonably good labor relations for about thirty years with the five public sector unions that represent the town's employees. Over the years, the changes in town officials had little impact on the labor relations picture. The town was relatively small, and most town officials knew the leaders of the public sector unions, all of whom were employees of the town.

Historically, the town and the unions negotiated two-year contracts, and the five labor contracts expired on the same date. Negotiations began in the spring and were generally concluded with all five unions before the June 30 expiration date. Over the past twenty or so years, it was the practice of the town to offer the identical wage increase and identical major fringe benefits to all the unions, and the settlements were almost always identical except for some minor benefits and work rules. Generally, the police union was the last holdout in the negotiations, but it almost always settled for what the other unions did.

In the spring of 1991, negotiations were started with the five unions for new contracts to be effective July 1, 1991. Unlike the negotiations that had occurred in 1989, the town's economic situation was grim. The nation was in a recession, and Granfield's unemployment rate was almost double that of the nation. The two major private employers had shut down, leaving all their former employees unemployed, and few of the private sector workers still employed received as much as a 2 percent wage increase in 1990 and 1991. Town revenues dropped substantially.

Because of the difficult economic situation, negotiations were not quite as smooth as in the past. Each of the five unions requested a 3 percent wage adjustment in each of the two years of the contract, with no other changes. The Town proposed a zero increase in 1991 and a 1 percent adjustment in 1992. After considerable negotiations, the town reached an agreement with the general municipal workers for a 2 percent adjustment on July 1, 1991, and a 1 percent increase on July 1, 1992, with no other contractual changes. Soon after, the other unions, except for the police, settled on the same terms. Some of the general public were enraged by these settlements. The mayor and other town officials received irate telephone calls, berating the town for agreeing to any wage increase. The local daily newspaper castigated the mayor for "caving in" to the unions' demands and inquired where the money for the wage adjustment was coming from.

Negotiations with the police union were still in progress after July 1, 1991. The police initially had set their goals on a 3 percent and a 2 percent wage settlement over the two years. However, in view of the general public hostility to the wage adjustments for the other public service unions, the police union backed down from its original demands, indicating a willingness to accept the settlement of the other public sector bargaining units. Now the mayor had doubts. She presented town data indicating that while the other town employees had their 2 percent wage increase funded in the previous fiscal year, there were no funds for a police wage increase in the new fiscal year. The union argued that this broke the precedent of uniformity of wage adjustments among the public sector unions. Clearly the opposition to the wage increase by the general public was the critical factor in the mayor's decision not to give the police union a wage increase. How were the parties to break this impasse?

Discussion Issues, Problems, and Questions

1. If you were the mayor, would you have refused to give the police union any wage increase? How would you have tried to settle the negotiations? What options would you have? In view of the public reaction to your settlement with the other public sector unions, how would you evaluate your chances for reelection?

2. If you were president of the police union, what would you do now to try to settle the contract dispute? Would you be willing to take a zero increase in the first year and a wage reopener in the second year of the contract? If you had the opportunity to start all over, would you have handled your negotiations differently?

3. As a voting citizen of the town of Granfield, do you feel that

none of the town employees should have gotten a wage increase in 1991? In view of the agreements reached between the mayor and the unions other than the police, should not the town live up to these settlements? If so, is it equitable to treat the police union differently? What do you suggest as a settlement of the dispute with the police union?

4. If you were president of the firefighters' local union that did reach an agreement on a wage increase, how would you react to the dilemma of the police union? If you thought the police should receive the same wage increase as the firefighters, would you openly support the police?

Case 4: The Effectiveness of Union Lobbying

Branville is a moderate-sized town in the Midwest with a few small industrial plants in and around it. It is about a one-hour commute from a large industrial city, and many of the townspeople hold jobs in the city. Branville is largely populated by middle-income blue-collar workers, many of them union members. In the public sector, all of the town's employees except for the teachers have been organized by unions, in five bargaining units, for about forty years.

In July 1989 a new superintendent of schools was hired, after the former one retired. The new superintendent was from outside the area, and his administrative experience was limited to a school system in a nonunionized area. By a variety of administrative moves in the first six months of his appointment the superintendent alienated a significant number of teachers. In a manner perceived by teachers as autocratic, he changed longstanding customs and practices. A number of teachers sought the assistance of the leaders of the other public sector unions, and a union organizing drive among teachers was begun. By early 1991 a teachers' union was certified as the bargaining agent for the school system of the town.

By the time the teachers' union and the superintendent began negotiations over a first contract, in June 1991, the other public sector unions had completed their contract negotiations with the mayor. Following a longstanding practice, the mayor had proposed a uniform package for all five of the bargaining units: 3 percent for the first year and an additional 3 percent for the second year of two-year contracts. The unions proposed a 5 percent increase in each of the two years, and after a few sessions with each union, two-year agreements were reached providing for 4 percent increases in each year. Minor nonwage adjustments were made in a few of the agreements.

At the first negotiation session of the teachers and the superintendent, the union president presented a draft proposal for a whole collective bargaining agreement. Having been coached and assisted by the leaders of the other public sector unions, the president was well prepared. The superintendent came to the session with an attorney who had little labor relations experience, and they were prepared only to talk about the wage issue. The parties exchanged proposals and agreed to meet again in two weeks.

At the second negotiation session, the union president made it clear that except for wages, its proposed contract contained provisions that formalized all of the existing benefits and the practices and procedures that had existed immediately prior to the arrival of the new superintendent. The wage proposal was a 6 percent increase in each of two years of a two-year contract. The superintendent submitted a written proposed wage adjustment of 3 percent in a one-year contract, with no change in all other aspects of employment conditions, including the rules he had instituted during his two years on the job. No progress was made at the session in resolving the differences.

In negotiating this first labor agreement, the union president realized that he had to achieve significant gains to show the union membership the benefits of organization. Getting the same size wage adjustment as the other public sector unions got would not satisfy the teachers. He conferred with the leadership of the other public sector unions and obtained their support; they too realized that if the teachers' union succeeded in obtaining more than a 4 percent wage adjustment, the other unions would have ammunition for a higher increase in the next round. The other unions attacked the school superintendent in the media as being antiunion and autocratic, and they whipped up considerable public support for the newly unionized teachers. In the numerous negotiating sessions that followed, the teachers held their ground, and the employer began to weaken. In early December the parties finally reached an agreement calling for a 5 percent increase in each of two years and all other aspects of the agreement as provided for in the union's original proposal. The union membership unanimously ratified the contract. The other public sector unions were very satisfied with the results of their lobbying activities and their intervention in the teachers' union negotiations with the school superintendent.

Discussion Issues, Problems, and Questions

1. As a voting citizen of the town, what do you think about the teachers' union settlement? Do you think the teachers should have gotten a higher wage adjustment than the other public employees? Do you feel that the school superintendent did an effective job in his negotiations with the union? Why or why not? Do you think the other public sector unions should have intervened in the teachers' union negotiations? Why or why not?
2. If you were president of the firefighters' union in the town, would you have advised the teachers' union to hold out for a wage increase higher than that received by the firefighters? Why or why not? If you would have advised the teachers to hold out, how would you have explained this to your own membership? Do you think your members would have condoned your lobbying for the teachers' wage increase?
3. How do you explain that the teachers were able to get more than the other public sector unions? Do you think the teachers' union president was a better negotiator than the other unions, or was the school superintendent a worse negotiator than the mayor? If the teachers' union had negotiated with the mayor rather than with the school superintendent, would the union have managed to get more than the pattern set for all the other unions?

Summary and Conclusions

There is little doubt and little argument that over the past thirty years, public sector employees and public sector unions have made significant long-term gains in benefits and membership growth, despite the fact that some states still do not authorize collective bargaining for their public employees. This growth has occurred as organization in the private sector has faltered, with membership in private sector unions declining in both absolute and percentage terms. Now, public sector union membership as a percentage of total government employment (membership density) is substantially higher than the equivalent figure for the private sector unions (35 versus 16 percent, respectively). In 1990 union membership in the public sector was about 30 percent of total union membership in the United States, although public sector employment represented only about 16 percent of the country's nonagricultural employment.

Prior to the 1960s the attitude of the general public, as well as of the legal community toward public sector unionization, was that public employment is a privilege, not a right, and that public employee collective bargaining somehow violated the democratic process of government. This does not mean that there were no public sector unions; many groups of public employees were organized into labor organizations and into professional associations with some characteristics of labor unions. However, these early organizations were prohibited by policy and law from engaging in collective bargaining. Their role was generally limited to lobbying for policies and legislation that would benefit their members. In many situations, these organizations were successful in obtaining benefits for their members, but it was generally through legislation or by lobbying before administrative agencies rather than the collective bargaining process. It was not uncommon to find post office employees, teachers, firefighters, and other public sector employees organized into labor organizations but with no legal authority to bargain over their wages and other terms and conditions of employment and no legal right to strike. The differences between public sector organizations and private sector labor unions were large and significant.

President John F. Kennedy's signing of executive order 10988 in 1962 appears to have encouraged collective bargaining in the public sector. Although this executive order was limited to federal employees, it had an impact on public sector employees outside the federal service. Many states subsequently enacted legislation that in a variety of ways granted public employees the right to organize and to bargain over a limited scope of terms of employment. Over the years, most states have enacted statutes granting all or some of their state and local employees the right to organize and to bargain collectively. Many of these statutes have placed limits on the scope of bargaining for the public employees within their jurisdiction, and some statutes have not granted all categories of public employees the right to organize and bargain collectively. Nevertheless, the collective bargaining rights of public sector employees and their labor organizations have expanded sufficiently to permit the growth of public sector unions.

In the public sector, the merit principle that government employees ought to be selected and retained solely on the basis of their qualifications for holding their jobs has prevailed for a long time. To administer this principle, most jurisdictions have established civil service commissions to oversee the merit system. Public sector collective bargaining is a bilateral form of decision making that frequently limits the prerogatives of the civil service commission, which prior to collective bargaining acted unilaterally. In many jurisdictions, collective bargaining and merit systems coexist, but they are often in conflict, and unions may rival civil service commissions in protecting employees against patronage politics. As the scope of collective bargaining widens, the prerogatives of the civil service commission become narrower. Employees generally prefer a process in which they participate directly, and this means they prefer collective bargaining over the civil service commission. In most jurisdictions outside the federal government, collective bargaining has become the main forum for public employees, and it has given the employees the protection that the civil service was initially designed to provide.

A number of questions arise concerning civil service versus collective bargaining. Have unions, through collective bargaining, implemented personnel rules contrary to merit principles? Is the system of civil service just another management tool? Is the civil service commission just another actor on the side of the public employer? Is it clear whether bargaining statutes take precedence over civil service statutes? Responses vary by individual and by state and community, and some responses undoubtedly change over time. In general, rules resulting from collective bargaining have not been contrary to merit principles. Civil service commissions have frequently been another participant on the management side in the rule-making process, and in some cases they appear to be a management tool. It is often not clear that statutes providing for collective bargaining take precedence over civil service statutes; court decisions have varied among the states, based largely on the language of the statutes.

Wages and monetary fringe benefits are central to a collective bargaining agreement. These are the items that most often cause a stalemate in negotiating. Nevertheless, they are not always within the bargaining scope for all public sector employees, just as they are not for classified federal government employees. Civil service salary structures are generally established by the legislature and may be changed or modified only by an act of the legislature. Unions affected by such a civil service salary structure have little choice but to seek changes in the structure through lobbying the legislature. Legislative changes do occur, but this is a far cry from negotiating a wage change through the direct collective bargaining process.

Certain monetary fringe benefits such as pension and insurance plans are frequently legislated statewide for all public service employees in the state, and these benefits remain outside the scope of collective bargaining. Vacations and holidays may also be excluded from the scope of bargaining. For some groups of public sector employees, specific items may be barred from the collective bargaining process. Despite these limits, it is not unusual to see public sector union organizations as militant as their private sector counterparts, and despite the illegality of public strikes, public employee unions have shown imagination and ingenuity in developing economic, political, and social pressures on public sector employers. As members of the general public, public employees participate in the process of electing public officials, and these officials are their employers who sit across the bargaining table. In many communities, the organized public employees and their families make up a sizable portion of the voting citizens. If they actively participate in the political process, the support of public employee unions may be critical in winning an election.

In most jurisdictions, the strike by public sector employees is illegal, and often a penalty may be specified. Nevertheless, strikes by public employees do occur, and frequently the penalty is waived or bargained away as part of the collective bargaining settlement. However, in some cases, severe penalties are imposed; the primary example was the strike of air traffic controllers in 1981. The federal government fired all controllers who engaged in what was an illegal strike against the federal government, and with rare exceptions they were barred from future employment with the federal government. But there were no such penalties for a 1970 postal stoppage.

Strikes by police or firefighters' unions are rare. Although the public attitude has apparently changed sufficiently so that some strikes by general public employees are tolerated, strikes by police officers or firefighters are not acceptable. (There probably have been insufficient strikes by these safety employees to test the hypothesis that the general public will not tolerate strikes by these employees. Nevertheless, the unions of these safety employees perceive the public as not accepting their striking and have developed other measures of pressures on public employers.) Political activity in local elections is a common measure used by all public service unions. More direct economic pressures, such as sick-outs or the blue flu, are not uncommon, although they are viewed as a poor substitute for the strike. Police unions are known to slow the issuance of parking violation summonses, reducing the town's revenues. In many jurisdictions, public service employees, especially police officers and firefighters, are covered by state statutes that provide fact-finding or binding arbitration where the parties have failed to reach an agreement on the terms and conditions of employment.

One study has summarized the issue of strikes in the public sector:

1. The average duration of strikes is shorter in the public than in the private sector.
2. State bargaining laws that contain strong strike penalties and highly structured impasse procedures . . . have reduced the number of strikes that might otherwise have occurred. . . .
3. The number of strikes by units of essential service employees has been lower in states with interest arbitration laws than in states where these units bargain under a fact-finding procedure or without a law.
4. The occurrence of strikes does not uniformly result in more favorable bargaining settlements for employees than occur in nonstrike situations or as a result of interest arbitration.
5. The occurrence of strikes does not uniformly endanger the public interest. Rather, the public welfare consequences of public employee strikes vary from nonexistent to very large.

In a few states, the economic strike by some public employees is legal in several ways (although not for public safety employees): a decision of the court, identified job classifications, and a limited period of strike as determined by legislature or the court. But even in these states, the number of strikes has been rather small; the general public attitude is often opposed to such action. Public sector unions have been relatively successful in winning many of their goals through the use of the political process instead of strikes.

The issue of the strike in public sector labor relations remains a persistent one and is generally held to be the major factor that differentiates labor relations in the public sector from the private sector. Although any strike may result in some discomfort to a party outside the dispute, the vast majority of public sector strikes have little impact on persons outside the local area. And despite the thousands of public sector collective bargaining negotiations that occur each year, relatively few are not settled between the two parties involved or with the assistance of a mediator or arbitrator. In the relatively few instances where an impasse is reached, there generally is a state law providing for fact-finding or arbitration as the next step in the process. In states where legislation provides for binding arbitration in public sector collective bargaining disputes, impasses rarely result in strikes.

Once a public sector union is recognized as the bargaining agent for a unit of employees, the next major step is negotiation over a collective bargaining agreement. Here the public employer must give up its unilateral authority to determine employment conditions and engage in a bilateral negotiation and determination of conditions of employment. If, as is fairly common, the public employer is negotiating with a number of unions representing a wide range of public employees, the picture is more complex. Different characters may represent management at different negotiations, sometimes leading to unexpected results. A school committee may negotiate with teachers, while the city council negotiates with the firefighters. A city manager or mayor may or may not participate directly, but their authority or political power may have an effect on the negotiations. In some cases, the civil service commission may claim authority over certain issues and thereby becomes a party to the negotiations. Generally the levels of compensation of various bargaining units differ, sometimes significantly. Frequently the public employer prefers granting a uniform change to all bargaining units, but negotiations of changes in compensation often become complex, as one or another of the unions informally (and sometimes formally) seeks to influence the negotiations of another union. In other situations, one union may take the lead in the bargaining process, with the other unions informally agreeing to follow. These situations can vary significantly from the normal bilateral negotiations.

Bargaining in the public sector has a number of other unique characteristics. It is not uncommon for a general public group to seek to influence the results of the collective bargaining process when it views its special interest as being affected. Property owners may view a wage increase for police officers as leading to higher property taxes. Parents of public school children may view an increase in class size as a decline in educational standards. Business groups may view an increase in the police outside detail rate as a tax on their business. In any of these situations, a group from the general public that perceives its interests as being affected by a collective bargaining negotiation may seek to intervene, directly or indirectly, in the bargaining process. Its weapon is generally a political threat, open or subtle, to the public employer of retribution at the polls. The success or failure of such intervention is somewhat determined by management's perception of the relative political strength of the special interest group relative to the political strength of the union involved.

Fiscal problems are another constraint that public management may face. What does a public employer mean when he or she tells the firefighters' union that the town cannot afford to grant the 5 percent increase proposed by the union? If the town had not granted a 6 percent increase to the police officers, would there have been sufficient funds to grant the 5 percent to the firefighters? If the town would grant sanitary workers only a 2 percent increase, would there be sufficient funds for the firefighters' 5 percent? If the town closed the public library two days a week, would there be sufficient funds for the firefighters' 5 percent? The town management has a number of alternative decisions it can make in order to satisfy the demand from one union. In most instances, there is no right or wrong answer. The public employer may make the decision based on perceived equity or political expediency.

In the private sector, few monetary fringe benefits that affect bargaining unit employees have been held to be outside the scope of collective bargaining. Management of private enterprises that have recognized a labor organization has given up considerable authority to the collective bargaining process, retaining those rights that may be subsumed under the general rubric of management rights. Illegal topics for negotiations would cover matters whose inclusion in a labor contract would violate some law or public policy. In the public sector, the picture is substantially different. Monetary fringe benefits for federal employees are not within the permissible scope of collective bargaining; they are mandated by law for all federal employees. Some monetary fringe benefit are within the scope of bargaining for state and local employees. There are variations in the coverage of scope among the various states, but most of the normally negotiated monetary fringe benefits are found in labor agreements involving state and local employees. Generally excluded from the bargaining scope for state and local employees are items such as health insurance, unemployment insurance, and retirement benefits, which are typically provided by statutes covering all public employees.

In the more than twenty years of the growth of unions and collective bargaining in the public sector, the vast majority of monetary fringe benefits covered by private sector labor agreements have gradually found their way into public sector labor agreements or into statutes with provision of these benefits. Just as there are variations in benefits among private industries, there may also be substantial differences among the various public sector bargaining units in a single community. A specific monetary fringe benefit that a police union may consider important for its members (court time) may be of minor importance to the teachers' union (class size). And what may be given considerable weight by a firefighters' union (staffing) may be of no significance to the clerical workers in the town hall (promotion). The specialized nature of these occupations may differentiate them from most occupational groups in the private sector. As a result, these groups may have specialized monetary fringe benefits on which they place a high priority.

Nonmonetary provisions in public sector collective bargaining are also sometimes limited by statute. A number of state laws specify certain exclusions from public sector bargaining. In some cases, the exclusions are general and apply to all public sector bargaining units; in other cases, the exclusions are specific and apply to specific employee groups.

Federal government employees are faced with the most limited scope in collective bargaining, where the law allows bargaining on the number, type, and grades of employees, work methods and technology, and the procedure for exercising managerial authority. For most state employees, state laws require bargaining over wages, hours, and important conditions of employment, while the issues of scope generally involve management rights. In the field of education, for example, scope issues of a nonmonetary nature include class size, decisions to grant or deny tenure assignments, schedules, and transfers from one school or subject to another. In some situations, these types of nonmonetary issues are specifically excluded from the scope of bargaining, while in others, the management rights provisions of the state laws may leave open the question as to whether such provisions are mandatory or permissible subjects for bargaining. Where such provisions are not specifically excluded from the scope of bargaining, teachers' unions often consider these provisions of the highest priority.

Because of the security nature of the duties of police officers and firefighters, many states impose legislative restrictions on their scope of collective bargaining. Some states specifically exclude the issue of minimum manning of shift coverage from collective bargaining for municipal police officers and firefighters. Although in general there is little difference between public and private sector agreements in matters such as union security, dues checkoff, or distribution of overtime, police and firefighters have many relatively uniform working conditions and situations that evolve into nonmonetary contractual provisions. Because of the nature of the work and the requirement of constant coverage, police and firefighters have work schedules and other work rules that vary significantly from those of other bargaining units in both the private and public sectors. Foreign service officers receive differential pay by post assignment. Overall, there are some significant differences that occur or exist between the public and private sectors. Some of these provisions exist because of the structure and administrative authority of the public sector employer and others because of the specialized duties, functions, and working conditions of employees.

The outcome of a collective bargaining negotiation normally depends on the relative bargaining power of the parties involved in the negotiation. There are no universal determinants of bargaining power. Factors that are commonly listed as having an impact on bargaining power include skill at bargaining, financial resources, the will to fight, and a host of institutional, political, and legal factors. In general, public policies affecting labor relations over the past fifty years have focused on equalizing the bargaining power of employers and unions within a framework defined by law. In the public sector, policies have also attempted to balance the right of employees to bargain over various conditions of employment with the protection of the public employer's interests.

Prior to the advent of the collective bargaining agreement in the public sector, most differences or disputes between employees and public management were handled through a civil service commission with administrative authority over the public merit system. The civil service commission established the rules of personnel administration in the public sector and was arbiter of disputes over its own rules and regulations. Once collective bargaining was introduced in the public sector, the role and authority of the civil service commission was modified. Where the law did not give final authority to the civil service commission or to collective bargaining, the system of dispute resolution was sometimes uncertain.

With or without a strong civil service system, most collective bargaining agreements in the public sector have incorporated a grievance procedure with final and binding arbitration. Thus, disputes arising under an interpretation of the collective bargaining agreement are normally handled and resolved through the grievance procedure established by the agreement. In some cases, accommodation with an existing civil service system is accomplished by establishing an independent and parallel procedure. In some situations a disciplined employee may resort to more than one appeals procedure, one after the other.

In the executive branch of the federal government, arbitration is required as the final step in negotiated grievance procedures, but arbitration awards are subject to review by courts or administrative bodies, or both. In a substantial majority of states, grievance arbitration is permitted or required in collective bargaining agreements involving public employees. However, because many states limit the scope of bargaining for some public employees, the grievance procedures negotiated by such employees are limited. With variation from state to state and from employee group to another, certain issues by statute or court decision are not within the scope of bargaining and therefore outside the scope of the grievance procedure and the jurisdiction of an arbitrator.

The basic issues arising in the grievance procedure of public employee bargaining are not significantly different from those arising in private sector grievances, and they generally are handled in the same fashion. The most common in both sectors are discipline and discharge, arbitrability, and just cause. Nevertheless, the specific issues that are raised in public sector grievance procedures are frequently more limited than in the private sector.

Disputes over the terms and conditions of employment are not easily or readily resolved in either the private or the public sector. In the private sector, such disputes are largely resolved through direct negotiations between the parties. The strike threat is always hovering, but its use has declined significantly over the past two decades. In the vast majority of jurisdictions, public sector employees have no legal right to strike. Nevertheless, even without the threat of a strike, the vast majority of public sector negotiations are resolved peacefully between the two parties. In some situations, an implied threat of an illegal strike or of withholding services in some fashion may be the factor that pushes the public employer to make concessions and arrive at a contract.

In both sectors, collective bargaining negotiations frequently need mediation, the help of an impartial person to assist the disputing parties to resolve their differences voluntarily. In the private sector, mediation has a long history where labor disputants agree upon an impartial third person to help the parties resolve a specific problem in impasse. In 1947 the Federal Mediation and Conciliation Service was established as an independent agency, with jurisdiction in disputes in the private sector as well as those involving federal employees. Mediation does not mandate resolution of a dispute, but it has become a widespread process in dispute resolution and also a successful one.

As state laws were enacted to authorize collective bargaining for public employees, many states created agencies whose principal purpose was to mediate disputes in the public sector. Although most contract negotiations are settled without outside assistance, a substantial number use mediation to assist in the resolution of disputes. And just as in the private sector, the mediation process is successful in the vast majority of instances where it is invoked.

Mediation, however, is not always invoked, or it fails to resolve the collective bargaining negotiations impasse. In the private sector, the threat of a strike or the strike itself helps resolve the dispute over the terms of a labor contract. Relatively rarely do the private parties in such situations use an arbitrator to determine the terms of a labor contract.

As a substitute for arbitration, the prearbitration procedure of fact-finding is used. The fact finder holds hearings and then issues a report with findings and recommendations, which are neither final nor binding. In many situations, the recommendations are the basis for a settlement or become the basis for further negotiations and a narrowing of the differences between the parties. Because of the strike option in the private sector, fact-finding is uncommon. However, in the public sector, fact-finding is fairly common and often is required by state statute.

In the public sector the general purpose of utilizing fact-finding in collective bargaining disputes is to place public pressure on the parties to accept the recommendations. Often, however, the parties delay serious negotiation until after the receipt of the fact-finder's recommendations. Since this process lacks finality, parties often view it as an intermediate step required to get to the procedure with finality—arbitration. Without the right to strike, most public service employees lack recourse to a process of final settlement of a labor contract. Fact-finding often, but not always, aids the parties. As a result, public employees' unions, especially those representing public safety employees, have lobbied for arbitration legislation.

Many state statutes mandate or permit public employees to take their contract disputes to arbitration. In some states, this right is specifically limited to police and firefighters, while some statutes remain silent on other public employees. Despite the finality of the arbitration process, there appear to be many problems in a number of public sector jurisdictions. State laws have been challenged in the courts on constitutional grounds involving either the relationship of the state to the local authority or the relationship of arbitration to the legislative process. An increasing number of state courts have upheld the constitutionality of interest arbitration in the public sector, but some problems remain. For example, when state legislation is silent on the matter of arbitration, is it then permissible for a public sector union to demand binding arbitration to resolve its contractual dispute? Is it permissible for the parties voluntarily to agree to binding arbitration in an interest impasse? If the legislation does not state that arbitration of contract terms is final and binding on the public employer, what happens if the city or town council refuses to fund the arbitration award?

Because of the political nature of public sector unions and collective bargaining, union goals are more likely to include the size of budgets and of employment than do the goals of private sector unions. As such items become part of the bargaining process, the employer is likely to view public employee labor organizations as more than mere unions concerned only with direct benefits for their members. The distinction between public sector and private sector unions is sharpened.

Similarly, there is a marked difference between public and private employers. In the public sector, bargaining power on the employer side is shared by both administrators and elected officials, and what often begins as a variant of private sector bargaining may end up as an extension of local politics. Unions and their members not only participate in the election of the public official with whom they must negotiate, but they also face other public groups that may participate on management's side in the collective bargaining negotiations. Unlike the situation in the private sector where bargaining is a bilateral process, public sector bargaining is frequently a multilateral process in which more than two distinct parties are involved in such a way that a clear dichotomy between the employee and management organizations may not exist.

Because of the nature of the services rendered by public employees, there is a much greater and personal interest by the general public in public sector union activities and collective bargaining than in private sector union actions. The service and performance of police and firefighters, teachers, and sanitation workers are of importance to the general public; at the same time, there appears to be a more direct tie between the benefits a public employee receives and the costs to taxpayers. Various interest groups in the general public give different weights and priorities to various services performed by the public employees, and therefore the costs of these services may be supported or opposed by different interest groups. Business groups that feel they need more and better police protection may be prepared to support higher pay for police officers. Families with children in the school system may support higher pay for teachers if they perceive that the higher pay will improve the education for their children. Older persons with no children in the school system may oppose higher pay for teachers if they believe higher taxes will result.

Since public sector management is frequently viewed as the person or persons representing the general public at the collective bargaining table, interest groups in the community often feel free to intervene in the bargaining process and sometimes actually participate with the official employer representative in the process. In many instances, there may be a fine line between intervention and participation; it is clear however, that special interest groups inject themselves into the process in order to tilt negotiations in their favor. When competing interest groups are involved, they may offset each other's leverage and pressures, leaving the result relatively uninfluenced by the special interest groups.

The complexities of public sector collective bargaining often leave the unions of public employees at a disadvantage compared to private sector unions. Private sector unions normally negotiate with representatives of management who have final authority to make a deal. In the public sector, however, multilateral negotiations are typical, and it is often difficult to determine where the final authority lies. The public sector union may be negotiating with a city manager, a mayor, a city council, the city treasurer, the finance committee, or any combination of them. In any specialized negotiations, additional participants may be called in as experts or as direct negotiators. In teachers' union negotiations, the superintendent of schools and members of the school committee are likely to participate on the employer's side. And in firefighters' or police negotiations, the fire chief or police chief is likely to participate on the employer side.

Final authority to fund any changes in an agreement may rest with someone or some group not directly involved in the negotiations. To the uncertain process is added the intervention of special interest groups of the community who have political clout with the direct participants. In addition, the members of the public employees' unions are voting citizens of the community, and the employer representatives sitting opposite the union representatives in the negotiating process may have been elected with the support of the union membership.

Despite the gains made by the public sector unions since the mid-1960s, recently there has been a significant slowdown in the gains made, and because of economic conditions, public employees have been laid off and unions forced to accept zero wage increases (although wage rate reductions are rare). External factors that could affect the public sector but not the private sector began occurring in the 1980s. Congressional actions suggest that states, cities, and towns are now required to pay a larger share of the bill for various public services. Programs have been reduced, and some are threatened with elimination. With such pressure, public sector unions are finding it more and more difficult to attain their goals. The opposition to tax increases has become widespread, and there are few ways to increase productivity of teachers, police, and fire-fighters without a drop in the quality of service. The public does not want a decline in the quality of public services, nor do they want an increase in taxes. The economic and financial pressures are likely to continue.

The concept of privatization of public services in order to reduce expenses has been introduced in a number of public sector services, and this may be the movement of the future as states and communities turn to private enterprise to perform the services that historically have been performed by public employees. If the issue of comparable worth comes to the forefront in many states, it could result in significant wage increases for female public employees, reducing employers' flexibility in allocating revenues. Cities have experienced significant increases in insurance premiums, putting financial pressures on many already hard-pressed communities. In addition, demographers indicate that early in the twenty-first century, large numbers of public employees will reach retirement age, yet public sector pension systems have been seriously underfunded. The future of public sector labor relations seems unstable.[2]

If economic and financial pressures on state and local budgets continue, probably there will be an increase of instability of labor relations in the public sector. As public employers are forced to reduce expenditures while being pressured to maintain the quality of services, public employee unions will be faced with employment cutbacks and wage cuts. Labor unrest is sure to follow, and with this unrest will come a greater amount of public intervention and participation in the collective bargaining process. Some pressure groups will be interested in maintaining quality services, others in maintaining or lowering costs. What is likely to result is bargaining on a broad political arena rather than collective bargaining between a union and an employer.

The public sector unions and public sector collective bargaining appear to face a grim future. There is renewed interest in public service and labor, and employment in the public sector is growing and is larger than in manufacturing. However, basic questions that had been raised in the past about public sector collective bargaining seem of little importance for the future of public service unions and collective bargaining. Should there be a federal law to regulate and prescribe labor relations programs for states and municipalities? Should state and local employees have the right to strike, subject to certain mediating and fact-finding conditions? The answers to such questions are not likely to change the picture of future instability in public sector labor relations.

There are, of course, actions and events that may revitalize the public sector unions and provide more growth opportunities. Unions could begin drives for favorable legislation in states that lack collective bargaining statutes. They could apply political pressure to change civil service commission laws and to liberalize collective bargaining and develop a more active political role in efforts to obtain favorable labor legislation. A change in the economic climate could result in more dollars being shifted to local services and thus improved opportunities for public sector unions. An increased public role in the health area would increase organizing opportunities for the public sector unions. Unions could move into more of the professional fields that appear to be growing in the public sector. Despite the current outlook for public sector unions and labor relations, the future is likely to present various opportunities for improvement.

Notes

Preface

1. John T. Dunlop, *Industrial Relations Systems* (New York: Holt, Rinehart, and Winston, 1958).

Chapter 1

1. For a detailed analysis of public sector labor legislation, see B. V. H. Schneider, "Public-Sector Labor Legislation—An Evolutionary Analysis," in Benjamin Aaron et al., eds., *Public Sector Bargaining*, 2d ed., Industrial Relations Research Association Series (Washington, D.C.: Bureau of National Affairs, 1988) pp. 201–202; and David Lewin et al., eds., *Public Sector Labor Relations*, 3d ed. (Lexington, Mass.: Lexington Books, 1988) pp. 326–329.
2. Schneider, "Public-Sector Labor Legislation," pp. 202–203.
3. David Ziskind, *One Thousand Strikes of Government Employees* (New York: Columbia University Press, 1940).
4. Ibid., pp. 3, 24–25.
5. Ibid., pp. 33–35, 54–62.
6. Sterling D. Spero, *Government as Employer* (New York: Remsen Press, 1948), p. 15.
7. As quoted by Jack Stieber, "Collective Bargaining in the Public Sector," in American Assembly, *Challenges to Collective Bargaining* (Englewood Cliffs, N.J.: Prentice-Hall, 1967), p. 80.
8. See ibid., pp. 79–84, for a discussion of these matters relating to government strikes.
9. Charles J. Coleman, *Managing Labor Relations in the Public Sector*, (San Francisco: Jossey-Bass, 1990), pp. 88–96.

Chapter 2

1. Philip Taft, *Organized Labor in American History* (New York: Harper and Row, 1964), pp. 27, 44–45.
2. Sterling Spero, *Government as Employer* (New York: Remsen Press, 1948), pp. 77–78.

3. Ibid., pp. 79–82.
4. Ibid., pp. 83–84.
5. David Ziskind, *One Thousand Strikes of Government Employees* (New York: Columbia University Press, 1940), pp. 24–25.
6. Spero, *Government as Employer*, p. 84.
7. Ziskind, *One Thousand Strikes*, pp. 25–26; Spero, *Government as Employer*, pp. 84–85.
8. Spero, *Government as Employer*, pp. 85–86.
9. Ziskind, *One Thousand Strikes*, p. 30.
10. Spero, *Government as Employer*, pp. 94–95.
11. Ziskind, *One Thousand Strikes*, p. 32.
12. Spero, *Government as Employer*, pp. 95–100.
13. Ibid., pp. 3, 16–20.
14. Ibid., pp. 105–109. Also see John Walsh and Garth Mangum, *Labor Struggles in the Post Office from Selective Lobbying to Collective Bargaining* (Armonk, N.Y.: M. E. Sharpe, 1992), pp. 43–56.
15. Spero, *Government as Employer*, pp. 110–133.
16. Ibid., pp. 228–237; Ziskind, *One Thousand Strikes*, pp. 52–71.
17. Spero, *Government as Employer*, pp. 245–257.
18. Ibid., pp. 257–288; Ziskind, *One Thousand Strikes*, pp. 39–51.
19. David Lewin et al., eds., *Public Sector Labor Relations: Analysis and Readings*, 3d ed. (Lexington, Mass.: Lexington Books, 1988), pp. 325–326.
20. Spero, *Government as Employer*, pp. 238–239.
21. Ibid., p. 215.
22. Ibid., p. 219.
23. Sar A. Levitan and F. Gallo, "Can Employee Associations Negotiate New Growth," *Monthly Labor Review* 112, no. 7 (July 1989): 5–14.
24. Richard F. Freeman and J. L. Medoff, *What Do Unions Do?* (New York: Basic Books, 1984), pp. 243–256. See also Derek C. Bok and John T. Dunlop, *Labor and the American Community* (New York: Simon and Schuster, 1970), pp. 312–317.
25. J. F. Burton, Jr., and T. Thowason, "The Extent of Collective Bargaining in the Public Sector," in *Public Sector Bargaining*, 2d ed., Industrial Relations Research Association Series, (Washington, D.C.: Bureau of National Affairs, 1988), p. 16.
26. J. Lelchook, *State Civil Service Employee Associations* (Washington, D.C.: U.S. Department of Labor-Management Services Administration, 1973), p. 5.
27. Levitan and Gallo, "Can Employee Associations," p. 12.
28. U.S. Department of Labor, Bureau of Labor Statistics, press release on bargaining activity in 1991, November 29, 1990.
29. B. V. H. Schneider, "Public Sector Labor Legislation—An Evolutionary Analysis," in *Public Sector Bargaining*, pp. 192–193.
30. Ibid., pp. 194–195.
31. J. L. Stern, "Unionism in the Public Sector," in *Public Sector Bargaining*, p. 55.

32. Schneider, "Public Sector Labor Legislation," pp. 195–196.
33. Ibid.
34. Stern, "Unionism," p. 56.
35. D. Lewin, "Public Employee Unionism and Labor Relations in the 1980's: An Analysis of Transformation," in S. M. Lipset, ed., *Unions in Transition* (San Francisco: Institute for Contemporary Studies, 1986), pp. 248–249.
36. B. Aaron, "The Future of Collective Bargaining in the Public Sector," in *Public Sector Bargaining*, pp. 314–315.
37. A. Anderson, "The Impact of Public Sector Bargaining," in A. Anderson and H. D. Jascourt, eds., *Trends in Public Sector Labor Relations*, vol. 1:1972–1973 (Chicago: International Personnel Management Association, 1975), p. 21.

Chapter 3

1. A. Anderson, "The Impact of Public Sector Bargaining," in A. Anderson and D. D. Jascourt, eds., *Trends in Public Sector Labor Relations*, vol. 1: *1972–1973* (Chicago: International Personnel Management Association and the Public Employment Relations Research Institute, 1975), p. 19.
2. I. B. Helbrun and N. D. Bennett, "Public Employee Bargaining and the Merit Principle," in Anderson and Jascourt, *Trends in Public Sector Labor Relations*, pp. 60–61.
3. See, for example, the collective bargaining agreement between the Portsmouth Naval Shipyard and the Federal Employee Metal Trades Council, AFL-CIO, 1985–1988.
4. The provisions of Chapter 589, of 1987, of the Commonwealth of Massachusetts established a Joint Labor-Management Committee with oversight responsibility for all collective bargaining negotiations involving municipal police officers and firefighters. The act provided that the factors to be given weight in any decision or determination shall include but not be limited to "the financial ability of the municipality to meet costs, determining such financial ability. Such factors which shall be taken into consideration include but not be limited to: (1) the city, towns, or districts' state reimbursements and assessments; (ii) . . . long and short term bounded indebtedness; (iii) estimated share, in the metropolitan district or commissioner's deficit; (iv) . . . estimated share of the Massachusetts Bay Transportation Authority's deficit; and (v) consideration of the average per capita property tax burden, average annual income of members of the community, the effect any accord might have on the respective property tax rates on the city or town."
5. J. Gyourko and J. Tracey, *Public Sector Bargaining and the Local Budgetary Process*, Working Paper 2915 (Cambridge, MA: National Bureau of Economic Research, 1989), p. 25.
6. S. Rosen, "Public Service Unions and Public Services," in W. D. Hawley and D. Roger, eds., *Improving the Quality of Urban Management* (Beverly Hills, Calif.: Sage Publications, 1974), pp. 564–565.

7. See Alice H. Cook, *Comparable Worth: A Case Book* (University of Hawaii at Manoa, Industrial Relations Center, 1985).

8. Ibid., p. 1.

9. Daniel J. B. Mitchell, "Collective Bargaining and Compensation in the Public Sector," in Benjamin Aaron, et al., eds. *Public Sector Bargaining*, 2nd ed., Industrial Relations Research Association Series (Washington, D.C.: Bureau of National Affairs, 1988), p. 152.

10. Cook, *Comparable Worth*, pp. 2–4.

11. A detail rate is the hourly rate paid to a police officer by a private firm or organization for police work outside the officer's normal duties. While set through collective bargaining, the detail rate involves no direct cost to the community.

Chapter 4

1. Henry B. Frazier III, "Federal Employment," in Public Employment Relations Services, *Portrait of a Process—Collective Negotiations in Public Employment* (Fort Washington, Pa.: Labor Relations Press, 1979), pp. 425–434.

2. Small units of private sector employees whose functions are found to be basically in intrastate commerce are not subject to the federal statutes. These employers would be covered by state law, which could be slightly or significantly different from the federal law. There are few large-scope employers in the private sector that are not covered by the federal law. Labor relations in railroads and airlines are covered by special federal legislation.

3. National Agreement between National Treasury and Employees Union and U.S. Customs Service, August 24, 1987.

4. Agreement between Portsmouth Naval Shipyard and Federal Employees Metal Trades Council, AFL-CI0, 1985–1988, p. 72.

5. See Bureau of National Affairs, *Digest of State Public Employee Bargaining Statutes* (Washington, D.C.: 1985).

6. Ibid., pp. 39–41.

7. Ibid., p. 49.

8. Ibid., p. 59.

9. Ibid., p. 97.

10. Ibid., pp. 105–106.

11. Ibid., pp. 121–122.

12. U.S. Department of Labor, Bureau of Labor Statistics, *Collective Bargaining Agreements for Police and Firefighters*, Bulletin 1885 (Washington, D.C.: Government Printing Office, 1976), p. 48, Table 19.

13. Ibid., p. 71.

14. Ibid., pp. 61–63.

15. Agreement between City of Boston and Boston Police Superior Officers Federation, July 1, 1979.

16. See U.S. Bureau of Labor Statistics, *Collective Bargaining Agreements*, pp. 43–44, for background.

17. Ibid., pp. 44–45.

Chapter 5

1. Charles J. Coleman, *Managing Labor Relations in the Public Sector* (San Francisco: Jossey-Bass, 1990), pp. 101–102.
2. Speech by Charles Cogen, July 8, 1965, quoted in M. H. Moskow, *Teachers and Unions* (Philadelphia: University of Pennsylvania Press, 1966), p. 216.
3. Moskow, *Teachers and Unions*, p. 217.
4. Laws of the Commonwealth of Massachusetts, chap. 589, 1987.
5. U.S. Department of Labor, Bureau of Labor Statistics, *Collective Bargaining Agreements for Police and Firefighters*, Bulletin 1885 (Washington, D.C.: Government Printing Office, 1976), pp. 37–39.
6. 1987–1989 Agreement between the Town of Westborough (Massachusetts) and the International Brotherhood of Police Officers, Local 439.
7. See, for example, Labor Agreement between the Town of Brookline (Massachusetts) and Brookline Branch, Massachusetts Police Association, July 1, 1988–June 30, 1991.
8. Labor Agreement between the Town of Brookline (Massachusetts) and Local 950, International Association of Firefighters, July 1, 1988–June 30, 1991.
9. Cleveland State University, Industrial Relations Center, *1990 Public Sector Collective Bargaining Agreements*, Report 9002-1 (July 1990), p. 47.
10. Ibid., pp. 36–37.
11. 1987–1989 Agreement between Town of Westborough and the International Brotherhood of Police Officers, Local 439.
12. Labor Agreement between the Town of Brookline and Local 950, International Association of Firefighters, July 1, 1988–June 30, 1991.
13. 1987–1989 Agreement between the Town of Westborough and the International Brotherhood of Police Officers Local 439.
14. Internal memorandum, "Report of Terms of Settlement," of Massachusetts Joint Labor-Management Committee for Municipal Police and Fire, February 8, 1991, the date the matter was removed from the agenda.
15. Commonwealth of Massachusetts, Acts of 1990, Chap. 100.
16. Cleveland State University, *1990 Public Sector Bargaining Agreements*, pp. 40–41.
17. Contract between the City of North Adams and the International Association of Firefighters, Local 1781, July 1, 1987 to June 30, 1990.
18. Agreement between Dartmouth Police Brotherhood and Town of Dartmouth, July 1, 1986–June 30, 1989.
19. City of Holyoke and International Association of Firefighters, Local 1693, July 1, 1985–June 30, 1988.
20. Agreement between the Town of Methuen and Local 1691, International Association of Firefighters, July 1, 1986–June 30, 1988.
21. Cleveland State University, *1990 Public Sector Bargaining Agreements*, pp. 42–43.
22. U.S. Department of Labor, *Collective Bargaining Agreements*, pp. 17–18.

Chapter 6

1. See Charles J. Coleman, *Managing Labor Relations in the Public Sector* (San Francisco: Jossey-Bass, 1990), pp. 134–137, for a detailed presentation of bargaining power.
2. David Lewin et al., eds., *Public Sector Labor Relations* 3rd ed. (Lexington, Mass.: Lexington Books, 1988), pp. 23–24.
3. Prior to this time, the U.S. Conciliation Service was part of the Department of Labor.
4. John T. Dunlop, *Dispute Resolution: Negotiation and Consensus Building* (Dover, Mass.: Auburn House Publishing Co., 1984), pp. 22–25. See also Sanford Cohen, *Labor in the United States*, 5th ed. (Columbus, Ohio: Charles E. Merrill Publishing Company, 1979), pp. 186–187.
5. David A. Dilts and William J. Walsh, *Collective Bargaining and Impasse Resolution in the Public Sector* (Westport, Conn.: Quorum Books, 1988), pp. 99–100.
6. Richard B. Freeman, "Unionism Comes to the Public Sector," *Journal of Economic Literature* 24 (March 1986): pp. 42–43.
7. Allen Ponak and H. N. Wheeler, "Choice of Procedures in Canada and the United States," *Industrial Relations* 19, no. 3 (1980): 305.
8. Craig A. Olson, "Dispute Resolution in the Public Sector," in Benjamin Aaron, et al., eds., *Public Sector Bargaining* 2nd ed., Industrial Relations Research Association Series (Washington, D.C.: Bureau of National Affairs, 1988), pp. 165–166.
9. See Joseph R. Grodin and J. M. Najita, "Judicial Response to Public-Sector Arbitration," in IRRA, *Public Sector Bargaining*, pp. 253–257.
10. Commonwealth of Massachusetts, Acts of 1980, Chap. 580, as amended sec. 4.
11. Tim Bornstein, "Interest Arbitration in Public Employment: An Arbitrator Views the Process," *Labor Law Journal* (February 1978): 85–86.
12. Coleman, *Managing Labor Relations*, p. 223.
13. Ibid., pp. 224–229.
14. See Richard A. Lester, *Labor Arbitration in State and Local Government* (Princeton, N.J.: Industrial Relation Section, Department of Economics, Princeton University, 1984).
15. For a thorough report of the early development and of its current mechanism of handling collective bargaining contract disputes for police and firefighters in Massachusetts cities and towns, see John T. Dunlop, "Commonwealth of Massachusetts Joint Labor Management Committee for Municipal Police and Fire," *Massachusetts Business and Economic Report* 8, no. 2 (Fall 1980), and transition statement, Joint Labor-Management Committee for Municipal Police and Fire, October 31, 1990, from John T. Dunlop, Chairman, to Massachusetts Secretary of Labor Paul J. Eustace.
16. *United Steelworkers of America v. American Manufacturing Co.*, 363 U.S. 564 (1960); *United Steelworkers of America v. Warrior and Gulf Navigation Company*, 363 U.S. 574 (1960); *United Steelworkers of America v. Enterprise Wheel and Car Corporation*, 363 U.S. 593 (1960).

17. Stanford Cohen, *Labor in the United States*, pp. 391.
18. Joseph R. Grodin and Joyce M. Najita, "Judicial Response to Public-Sector Arbitration," in IRRA, *Public Sector Bargaining*, pp. 247–249.
19. Ibid., pp. 262–263.
20. Coleman, *Managing Labor Relations*, pp. 144, 152.
21. As quoted in ibid., p. 145.
22. Ibid., p. 154.

Chapter 7

1. Charles J. Coleman, *Managing Labor Relations in the Public Sector* (San Francisco: Jossey-Bass, 1990), p. 16.
2. Harry T. Wellington and Ralph K. Winter, Jr., *The Unions and the Cities* (Washington, D.C.: Brookings Institution, 1971), p. 202.
3. Richard Freeman, "Unionism Comes to the Public Sector," *Journal of Economic Literature* 24 (March 1986): 4.
4. Ibid., p. 44.
5. Thomas A. Kochan, "A Theory of Multilateral Collective Bargaining in City Governments," *Industrial and Labor Relations Review* 27, no. 4 (July 1974): 526.
6. John F. Burton, Jr., and Terry Thomason, "The Extent of Collective Bargaining in the Public Sector," in *Public Sector Bargaining*, 2d ed. (Industrial Relations Research Association Series (Washington, D.C.: BNA, 1988), p. 37.
7. Howard Block, "Criteria in Public Sector Interest Disputes," in *Arbitration and the Public Interest*, Proceedings of the Twenty-fourth Annual Meeting, National Academy of Arbitrators (Washington, D.C.: BNA Books, 1971), p. 173.
8. David Lewin, et al., eds., *Public Sector Labor Relations*, 3d ed. (Lexington, Mass.: Lexington Books, 1988), p. 543.
9. Ibid., p. 544.
10. Commonwealth of Massachusetts, Acts of 1987, Chap. 589, sec. 3A.
11. Ibid.
12. Milton Derber, "Management Organization for Collective Bargaining in the Public Sector," in *Public Sector Bargaining*, pp. 90–94.
13. Coleman, *Managing Labor Relations*, p. 296.
14. Ronald Donovan and Marsha J. Orr, *Subcontracting in the Public Sector: The New York State Experience*, Institute of Public Employment Monograph 10, (Ithaca: New York State of Industrial and Labor Relations, 1987), pp. 1–2.

Chapter 8

1. David Lewin, et al., eds., *Public Sector Labor Relations*, 3d ed. (Lexington, Mass.: Lexington Books, 1988), p. 588.
2. Ibid., pp. 582–583.

Index

Ability to pay, 40–41, 120, 176, 189–4
AFL-CIO, 61
Air traffic controllers, strike of, 116, 173
Alcoholism
  drug testing and, 93–95
  rehabilitation programs for, 95–96
American Arbitration Association, 130
American Association of University Professors, 22
American Federation of Labor (AFL), 18–19
Metal Trades Department of The (AFL), 17
American Federation of State, County and Munic-
    ipal Employees (AFSCME), 20, 43
American Federation of Teachers, 83
Arbitral finality, principle of, 126
Arbitration, 59, 115, 117–25
  conventional, 121, 122
  fact-finding as intermediate step to, 118, 181
  final-offer, 121, 122
  as final step in grievance procedure, 8, 127,
      130, 179
  interest, 26, 114–15, 116, 117, 118, 120–21,
      181
  last-best-offer, 123, 124
Arbitration awards, 155
  refusal to fund, 139–40
Army arsenals, strikes by workers in, 16
Atomic Energy Labor Relations Panel, 113
Attitude toward unions in public sector, public,
      19, 20–21, 170, 173–74
Authority
  of funding, governmental, 11
  uncertainty of line of, 3, 183

Bargaining. *See* Collective bargaining; Scope of
      bargaining
Bargaining power, 110, 178, 182
Bargaining unit(s), 5, 7, 8
  dealing with multiple, 151–52
  diversified, 25
  uniform settlement with all, 152, 153, 175
Benefits. *See* Monetary fringe benefits; Nonmone-
      tary contractual provisions
Benevolent associations, 18–19, 21. *See also*
      Police officers
Block, Howard, 152
Board of Conciliation and Arbitration, Massachu-
      setts, 122, 145
Boston, Massachusetts
  police strike of 1919, 3, 18, 19, 20
  struggle for 10-hour day in, 14–15

Brooklyn navy yard, 15
Budgets, 151, 181
  economic and financial pressures on state and
      local, 183–84
  impact of, 27–28, 134–36
Bureau of Labor Statistics (BLS), 23, 33, 37–38

Cancer presumption act, Massachusetts, 92–93
Cap on work hours, 98–99
Charlestown, Massachusetts navy yard, 1852
  strike at, 15
Cincinnati, 1918 police strike in, 2
City council, 35, 54–57
Civil liberties, no-smoking rules and, 91
Civil rights, public sector union movements and,
      22
Civil Service Act of 1883, 18, 23
Civil service commission, 8, 10, 110–11, 171–72,
      179
Civil service merit system, 35–36, 110–11,
      171–72
Civil Service Reform Act, 26, 127
Civil War, 16
Classified positions, 6, 31, 61
Clinton, Bill, 33
Collective bargaining, 8, 23–27
  dispute resolution and, 110–11
  evolution of, 22, 23–25
  executive order 10988 and, 22, 24–25, 30, 171
  merit systems and, conflict between, 110–11,
      171–72
  outlook for public sector, 184–85
  political process versus, 11–12
  recent developments in, 25–27
  scope of. *See* Public intervention in public sector
      bargaining; Scope of bargaining
Communities
  pattern of settlements in, 38–39
  public employees as voting citizens of, 150, 183
Comparability to private employee wages, stan-
      dard of, 31–32
Comparable wages in comparable communities,
      39–40
Comparable worth, 42, 157–58, 184
"Concerted activities," right to engage in, 1
Constitutionality of interest arbitration, 118, 181
Consumer Price Index (CPI), 37
Contractual provisions, nonmonetary. *See* Non-
      monetary contractual provisions
Conventional arbitration, 121, 122

About the Author

Morris A. Horowitz is a labor economist with a B.A. degree from New York University and a Ph.D. from Harvard University. He began his career with the U.S. Department of Labor, and then worked for the National War Labor Board during World War II, and with the Wage Stabilization Board during the Korean War. He was a researcher and professor at the Institute of Labor and Industrial Relations at the University of Illinois for four years. He was Research Associate in Labor at Harvard University for three years. He has been a professor of economics specializing in labor and industrial relations at Northeastern University in Boston for the past 35 years, and has written numerous articles and books in the labor field. He has served as a labor consultant to the Ford Foundation and to the International Labor Organization in a number of Latin American countries. Horowitz has been a part time arbitrator and mediator in the labor relations field for the past 40 years. He has served as arbitrator under a number of collective bargaining agreements and has issued several hundred awards. He is a member of the National Academy of Arbitrators. Since 1979 he has been serving as Vice-Chairman of the Massachusetts Joint Labor–Management Committee for Municipal Police and Fire. He is currently Professor of Economics Emeritus at Northeastern University.